SOUNDINGS

REFLECTIONS FROM A HUSBAND, FATHER, AND FINANCIAL PLANNER.

SOUNDINGS

REFLECTIONS FROM A HUSBAND, FATHER, AND FINANCIAL PLANNER.

JON KAGAN, CFP®

Jon Kagan, CFP®

SOUNDSIDE WEALTH ADVISORS
7552 Navarre Pkwy Unit 35
Navarre, FL 32566-7309

T 850.936.6686
F 850.936.8816
https://soundsidewealth.com/contact/
https://soundsidewealth.com/

Soundings, Jon Kagan —1st ed. ISBN 978-1-955242-91-2

To Kathleen, Alex & Collin. Thanks for allowing me to share the good, the less-than-good, and the zany, for all these years...

CONTENTS

2016

2017

2018

INTRODUCTION

Life is a trust business. Depending on your nature, you either start with it, or you don't. Your perspective is based on the experiences of your life. How you were raised; where you were raised; was there spirituality; what was your education; who were your friends. All of these factors, and countless others, go towards your world view and most importantly for the purpose of this discussion, your initial predisposition to enter a relationship with trust or skepticism.

There are several reasons that I put this book together. Very soon, you'll read how it began, from a monthly newsletter created mid-year in 2008, carried forward to this day. The purpose of the newsletter was to educate, entertain, and to give the reader a peek into my beliefs, so that over time, they'd understand where I was coming from so they could decide if there was a basis for a long-term relationship.

Over the years, to my great surprise, people shared how much they enjoyed their monthly Soundings. What amazed me the most was the breadth of the fanbase. Men, women, young, elderly. It was like the old theme song from Armour Hot Dogs and it was truly humbling. Most admitted that they turned right to the back page, titled, "On a Personal Note", where I shared the highlights of the previous month from the perspective of a husband and father of two young sons, trying to figure it all out together, and making lots of mistakes along the way. I hoped that one day, I'd compile the years of the back page, into a tome to pass to friends and family.

This project started out as just that, but as I reviewed the years of history, I realized that it might be useful to others going through all of life's craziness. We've all heard the quote from Mark Twain, "History doesn't repeat itself, but it often rhymes." So many of the issues of the past, that I tried to report on humorously through the lens of my family, still exist today (imagine that?!) The rocky road on which we currently tread was just as bumpy back then. And yet, here we are, still chugging along, quite probably the better for it...fire tempers steel, doesn't it?

So here we go. I hope you enjoy the pages to come. It was a labor of love, and it continues on a monthly basis.

2008

Introduction to the First Newsletter: May 2008

Hello everyone. I'd like to humbly introduce you to the first edition of our new monthly newsletter. I just returned from the 2008 Raymond James National Conference for Professional Development where I had the opportunity to hear from some world class minds in the area of finance, economics, money management and estate planning. One of my favorite parts of these events is the opportunity to hear from top advisors at breakout sessions where they share tips on what they've learned and how they've evolved their practices over the decades. On marketing, one participant shared his monthly newsletter and told of the "back page", a personal section where he shares the latest goings on of his family. He spoke of meeting a long-time client for the first time in-person. She walked up, gave him a huge hug, and said, "I love you." It was the result of truly getting to know him and his family over the years, warts and all, from the open and personal notes in his monthly newsletter.

So here we begin, with the first edition of our version. In days gone by, a ship's officers took Soundings to aid in the safe navigation during a journey. I've named our monthly newsletter the same with the hope it will provide you with timely information that will help you better navigate your next adventure.

May 2008

"The only limit to our realization of tomorrow will be our doubts of today."

Franklin D. Roosevelt

Kathleen, my much better half, travelled to Orlando to attend niece Kate's college graduation. I was out of town at a business conference, so our good neighbors volunteered to tend to our boys, Alex and Collin, for the weekend. Of course, I was counting on them to be on good behavior, but you never know. Well, I got a call on Saturday morning from Gina who reported the boys were wonderful. She told them that they were so well behaved because their mother was so strict. They quickly corrected her, saying their dad was the tough guy, not mom. I was so proud I gave them a day off from the coal mines and let them sleep in till 4:30am on Sunday.

December 2008

"The function of economic forecasting is to make astrology look respectable."

John Kenneth Galbraith

A couple years back, I opened an investment account for Alex and Collin, who were 9 and 11 at the time. I seeded it with little cash and made a deal with them. Any time they'd add money to their investment, I'd match it. I sweetened it up by agreeing to add to it when their report card made the Honor Roll. Finally, I had them defer ½ of their allowance and printed up a spreadsheet showing them how their systematic savings should give them enough to buy their first car sometime down the road (maybe even something nicer than $50 1971 Oldsmobile Delta 88 hand-painted (by me) in flat black primer. For the first year, it was fun and exciting to show them how their investment had grown and talk to them about the stocks that were in their mutual fund. Well, it's been less fun this year now that their aggressive mutual fund is down over 40% and worth less than the all the money they've put in over the years. When I told Alex he needed to invest the money he received from his Nana for his birthday in October, he was less than enthused and said, "why bother when it just keeps going down?" The "wise guy" taught me that aversion to loss is hard-wired at a young age. I then taught him about "buying low and selling high", the virtues of thinking long term, and most importantly, the fact that our house is NOT a democracy. If I tell him something's a good idea, it IS a good idea!

Thanksgiving has come and gone, and it afforded another good teaching opportunity in light of the tough economic times. We had a solid family talk about the economy and the fact that many people are losing their jobs at the holiday season. Add in the fact that those who are most vulnerable and reliant on the giving of others may be finding that giving isn't as plentiful as in years' past. To that end, when we received solicitation from a local shelter for money to feed the homeless at Thanksgiving, our boys made us proud when they volunteered some of their own "treasure".

2009

200

April 2009

"I am an optimist, unrepentant and militant. After all, in order not to be a fool an optimist must know how sad a place the world can be. It is only the pessimist who finds this out anew every day."

Peter Ustinov

A couple weeks back, a very dear client passed away. She was 88 years old and passed peacefully in her sleep but I will miss her a bunch. She was a Harvard trained Botanist, and with her husband (a fellow Botanist and former Professor of hers), they travelled the world conducting research and publishing cutting edge materials that advanced their field. The reason I bring her up is because her death marks a new beginning for her and her husband's legacy. Together, we designed an estate plan that will ensure their life's work will continue. One of the provisions we implemented was an endowed scholarship to the University of Wisconsin (where she earned her Undergraduate and Master's degrees) for a woman to enter into the field of science. For those of you that haven't put your estate in order, I promise it's a liberating experience.

Last weekend, my Rotary Club held its 2nd Annual "Running Wild 5k". Last year, we ran wild for our local zoo with the proceeds going towards some much needed renovation. This year, we ran wild for education...the proceeds funding scholarships for some deserving local high school seniors. While "carbo-loading" the night before at our favorite pizza joint, "Sal's" in Navarre (you'd have to go to NJ to get pizza this good), I told my boys my goal was to break 25 minutes. My "trash-talking" teen and preteen went on to share their opinion that I don't have a chance. We decided a wager was in order and given the slow economy has taken away both their allowance and my disposable income, we thought of a wager far better than money. We decided the loser(s) would be required to wear a pair of clip-on earrings to school or work depending on the identity and vocation of the loser(s). With the "game on" we called it a night amidst continued taunting by my trash-talkers. The next morning, we awoke to perfect running weather, sunny and in the upper 50's with just a slight crosswind. I am happy to report a time of 23:30, my best run since 1994 (Kathleen records this stuff). The boys looked beautiful that night at dinner in their huge, dangly, gold-colored ear bling!

June 2009

/////▬▬▬/▬▬▬▬▬▬▬▬/▬▬▬/////▬▬▬▬▬▬/▬▬▬▬▬▬▬▬

> *"May your hands always be busy, may your feet always be swift; May you have a strong foundation, when the winds of change shift."*
>
> Bob Dylan

We're doing our best to prevent our kids from being among the 36% in our county that are at risk for obesity according to a recent story released by our Health Department. Thursday was the last day of school and we have a formal TV policy. The tube goes off at 10:00 am and stays that way until 4:00 pm. What is allowed during that prime time is bike riding, ball playing, reading, guitar playing, skate-boarding, weed-pulling, fort building, and even girl-chasing. Collin is out there pulling weeds as I write.

Collin, true to his birth order, is afraid of nothing (except the dark and the boogeyman…but who isn't?). After some solid (lucky) trouble-shooting, I was able to get our old boat running over the weekend and told the boys I'd take them wakeboarding. When it was Collin's turn, Kathleen noticed his shorts, hand-me-downs from his older cousin, were at least two sizes too big and wouldn't stand a chance of staying up while getting pulled behind the boat. Not wanting to miss out and not missing a beat, he dropped the baggy shorts and skied in his skivvies. I have no doubt that if Collin happens to graduate college during a rough economy, he will adapt, improvise, and overcome any challenge that comes his way.

August 2009

"The trouble with life isn't that there is no answer, it's that there are so many answers."

Ruth Benedict

T he Fourth of July was a little more somber this year since a dear friend and client of ours passed away. Howard was about as all American as it gets. Born in Ohio, he enlisted in the Navy, worked his way up the ladder before retiring as a Chief Petty Officer. He made his way back home to Ohio and got hired on by the local Ford plant. True to his nature, when he received his first paycheck, he couldn't believe how generous it was and thinking there was a mistake, was going to take it back if not stopped by his sister who told him everything was as in order. I met Howard and his wife Phyllis after he had retired from Ford and they settled in Florida. Even though heart disease had slowed him down, he was as sweet a man as you'd ever meet and greeted everyone with a big, warm smile and me with a firm handshake that'd always bring an only half-joking grimace to my face. Howard left his wife Phyllis, step-kids Michael and Juli, grandson Jackson, and me, with an example of how nice-guys don't have to finish last and how successful you can be in life with love, compassion, and a positive attitude.

September 2009

"Maturity is the capacity to endure uncertainty."

John Huston Finley

The boys are back in school, knocking out homework and in the middle of Football season. It's their second year in the sport and we're having a lot of fun this season. The scary part is that as they get older and bigger, so does the weight limit and right now the boys in their league can max out at 200 lbs. about what Alex and Collin weigh together! You can feel it in the stands when someone takes a good hit. The saving grace for us as parents is that our boys are more gifted in the academic pursuits than in athletics so the risk of them getting hurt has been mostly limited to butt-splinters.

October 2009

I chose this month's quote to frame our upcoming seminar on Estate Planning. What would happen to your family if you didn't come home today? Understandably, most of us don't want to think about it and by default take for granted that things will work out. Estate planning is not just something wealthy people do to make sure the favorite nephew gets the beach house. It's about making sure your family is taken care of if, God forbid, you have a premature departure. Among the topics to be discussed, we'll cover the various legal documents and how they are used in estate planning, how the laws are changing and what effect it could have on your existing documents, and things to consider when choosing an executor or trustee.

September 16th marked the five-year anniversary of Hurricane Ivan, an event that changed all our lives down here in the greater Pensacola area. It would be too easy to tell a bummer of a story, so I thought I'd share a funny one.

About five years prior to the storm, we found an older house in rough shape, but on a beautiful lot on the water. It had been vacant for nearly two years and as we cleaned the cockroach droppings from the pantry closet, I did my best to comfort Kathleen, who was wondering out loud what we had gotten ourselves into. I assured her everything would work out and we'd made a great investment. Privately, I remember thinking the best thing that could happen would be a hurricane so we could just start over. Fast forward five years…our house had been transformed into a home with a bunch of love and gallons of sweat equity. With Hurricane Ivan about 8 hours away, I made a final walkaround to check on the boards I put up around all the south-facing windows. At that time, I noticed that where the old outdoor showerhead protruded from the siding, there was room for a driving rain to work its way in. We couldn't have that; it might lead to some longer-term wood rot problems, so it was off to Lowes to get some caulk for a quick repair. Talk about a case of monumental underkill; when we were able to get back home the day following the storm, the back of the house was now in the front yard along with most of our "stuff". The good news is our insurance came through, we learned that "stuff" can be replaced, and to value what can't.

Me and Pop

Easter Empty Nest

The boys

Alex and Claire

Travel Adventures

2010

January 2010

"We must welcome the future, remembering that soon it will be the past; and we must respect the past, remembering that it was once all that was humanly possible."

George Santayana

I hope you all had a wonderful Holiday… ours was full of family, both immediate and extended and in the interest of space, I'll spare you the details but I will tell you that our son Alex surprised me with the gift of all gifts, a new pink "snuggie" after he remembered my comments one night watching tv. I'm sure it will one day be as big a collectors' item as a Popeils' Pocket Fisherman or Ronco Bass-a-Matic 76, but in the meantime, I've got to say it sure has been nice during the recent sub-freezing temperatures, watching the all the football games wrapped in pink warmness. I'll leave you all with that frightening vision.

February 2010

Thomas Alva Edison was the epitome of perseverance. His light bulb, perfected in 1879, was an ultimate success only after years of trial and error. But Edison was a man of unique perseverance and unbending will. After countless failed attempts to find the right material from which to compose the filament, he was famously quoted, "I have not failed, I've just found 10,000 ways that won't work."

A big milestone was reached in the life of our eldest son Alex...his first girlfriend. It was a less-than-stormy affair (good since he's only 14), the deal was sealed when his friend took cell phone, pretended to be Alex, and made the arrangement via a text message. Alas, young love is a bit fickle and on the eve of their one-week anniversary, a text from his new beau brought the relationship to an end. Welcome to the world my son.

Collin's is more focused on sports now and is back on "Round ball" courts causing fear and awe in all on the opponent's bench. We always liked watching our scrappy youngest on the basketball court and are happy to see him back after a three-year hiatus, especially since his growth spurt has made him one of the taller kids out there. So far, they are 4 and 1 and number one in their division, but that of course makes them a big target and there's still plenty of season left.

March 2010

"Behold the turtle. He makes progress only when he sticks his neck out."

James Bryant Conant

I knew it would come sooner or later; I just thought it would be further out on the "later" end of the spectrum. Last year, our then 13-year-old son Alex and I had a photo finish at the Navarre Rotary 5k. I squeaked out victory by a nose, which in my case is about 1 ½ a horse length. Fast forward to last weekend when we ran the Navarre YMCA "Give your Heart to the Kids" 5k, on a cold, windy and overall nasty Saturday morning. As always, we set out together and weaved our way through the masses after the starting horn was blown. But this year, when we settled into our rhythm and Alex said, "this feels like a good pace dad," I had to tell him to go for it while I downshifted into 'old, fat-man gear.' At the time, I still had the false confidence that I'd catch him in the last mile or so after he burned himself out but that never happened and the son-of-a-gun beat me by just under 2 minutes! It's the beginning of something I'm not quite sure I'm ready for.

Over the summer, #2 son Collin was talking with his Aunt Carrie about school and how he was an A/B student. Carrie, in the running for mother-of-the-millennium, had none of it and told Collin that he was absolutely an A student and needed to hold himself to that standard. Of course, she was right, he bought it (coming from someone other than his parents who, after all, really don't know so much) and so far, this year, Collin has yet to bring home anything other than "A's" on his report card. I'm thrilled but it's costing me an extra $50 each semester since I put $100 into his investment account for every all-A report card vs. just $50 for an A/B version.

I normally just embarrass my kids in this section but I will turn the spotlight on myself for a paragraph. I had a very special and highly personal day on February 25th that I will share with the hope that maybe someone else out there will go for a repeat. For all the normal reasons, I was estranged from my father for the past 12 years or so. It was a very typical case of family dysfunction with the major symptom being that of stubbornness and the fact that long distance made it easy to just take the path of least resistance and do nothing. Well, I'd thought about it for several days and decided to call my dad on his birthday just to wish him a happy day and tell him I loved him. We ended up having a very nice conversation which opened the door to future conversations and I've got to say that when I got off the phone, I hadn't felt that good in a long time. Take it for what it's worth, every family has issues and sometimes we let the silly things override what is important in life but if you didn't wake up tomorrow morning, is there someone out there that you wish you'd have reached out to one more time? If so, what do you have to lose?

April 2010

"Everything that can be invented has been invented"

Charles H. Duell

I told you last month that Alex put the hurt on me in the Navarre YMCA 5k, breaking the tape a whopping two minutes before his tired old man. Not ready to admit a permanent unseating, I was looking forward to a rematch this morning at our 3rd annual Navarre Rotary 5k. This time, Collin joined the fun as well as Dustine Emerson (my Navarre High School mentee and his younger brother William). It was a beautiful morning, a perfect 60 degrees with a nice refreshing crosswind and I was ready to gain back the title of Kagan family "alpha male". It was a nice thought anyhow. Not only did Alex crush me by nearly three minutes, but Collin took me out by 2 and Dustine took us all down by finishing in 5th place overall. I guess it's only a matter of time before they're changing my diapers and feeding me too.

May 2010

There we were, a beautiful spring evening, with light breeze out of the north, under a crescent moon. The final inning of the game with us down 5-4, after the opposing team managed to rally at the top of the inning. With bases loaded and two outs, Collin stepped up to the plate. As if the pressure wasn't enough, his buddies were ten feet up and behind him working the score board along with big brother Alex. The tension was palpable as the first pitch came in fast…Strike! Undeterred, or so we choose to believe, Collin choked up on the bat and performed his new pre-pitch ritual…too detailed and secret for this missive. The next pitch…another fastball down the pipe but this time Collin would not be denied. Crackkk!! A high drive, beautifully placed over the third baseman's head and down the left field line…two men score, Collin is on second. We'd go on to win 10 – 4 (with the six-point rule ending the game). Ah, the field of dreams…

July 2010

"Nothing in life is to be feared. It is only to be understood"
Marie Curie

Given all the distressing news lately, topped locally by our awful situation in the Gulf of Mexico, I keep thinking of Lloyd Bridges character in the timeless classic, Airplane, as he laments how he picked the wrong week to stop sniffing glue. As Madame Curie suggests in the quote above, a more constructive approach is to examine what's taken place to get an understanding of the why's, the how's and the what might be next's, in order to formulate a reasonable approach to move forward.

You may have felt like the Earth had shifted slightly off its axis recently. We had a little Kagan Dysfunctional Family Reunion at our place. My youngest brother Josh, the wildest of three Kagan boys, a one-time bass player in a punk rock band and author of the anthem to the hernia, "guts in my nuts"; his wife Krys, an accomplished cook and author of a food blog with fans from all around the world; and their two boys Arthur and Adam (1 ½ and 3 ½) came over from Austin, TX. My mom made the trip northwest from the NY coast of Florida...Sarasota. We had a great time chasing those youngins' around and sampling my sister-in-law's cooking. She really knows her way around the kitchen. The twist is that she keeps a Vegan household so we got to try some things that I never even knew were edible...who knew you could eat kale? In case you didn't know, Vegans don't even drink milk...I don't get that part, won't a cow eventually explode if you don't milk it? We had a wonderful time, mostly just taking it easy outside and given that we Kagans are a quite a pasty white bunch, I think Coppertone sales are going to show a big rise next quarter.

Speaking of Collin, his team had their Dizzy Dean State baseball tournament this weekend. Game one was a nail-biter going over three hours but, in the end, they pulled off a stunning 11 – 10 victory. It was Collin's one and only game of the tournament because at his first at bat, he got a hit but broke his hand in the process. Since we had no subs and we didn't know for sure it was broken, he played the whole game making another hit and a beautiful running catch in left field. That high threshold for pain will really help out later in married life.

August 2010

"Wherever we look upon this Earth, the opportunities take shape within the problems."

Nelson Rockefeller

You always hope that your kids will have more than you did (don't you?). While I waited in vain for the growth spurt that never came, my boys continue to grow like weeds. Collin, who just turned 13 in May, has now overtaken me as the altitude king of the family. Don't get me wrong, I can still take him, but I can now call on him to get the things from the top shelf of the cupboard beyond the reach of my stubby little digits. And while sitting on the couch watching tv a few weeks back, I looked over at the young lad's leg and had to shake my head. I don't know where it came from but he had an adult model complete with hair and a big ol' Shaquille O'neal looking foot on the end. Who IS this kid?

And Alex, our one-time shy and introspective oldest is heading to High School this August. I mentioned one-time shy because it seems he may have turned the corner on that one. We were out at the beach a couple weekends back at Jimmy Buffet's new burger joint, the Land Shark Landing (great fun by the way...good burgers, cold beer for mom and dad, live music every night, and fun stuff for the kids on the sand while you're waiting for your order). When our burgers arrived and the kids came back from the beach, Alex was texting away on his phone. It seems he met some tourist girls staying at the adjoining hotel and he scored some digits… kid talk for a phone number. It turned out my "ladies' man" spent the rest of the weekend texting his new friends and trying to convince us to take him back to the beach to hang out. Where'd THIS kid come from?

September 2010

"A man is but a product of his thoughts; what he thinks, that he becomes."

Mahatma Gandhi

Watching the video of the 33 Chilean miners trapped deep inside the Earth, the timeline already at 21 days and faced with the prospect of another 3 – 4 months, I thought of this quote from Gandhi. When the specially designed camera was lowered 2200 feet into their granite prison and the video streamed to the world and their anxious families, it showed a scene of jubilation, even as the men were given the tough news that they were looking at some serious time down there. Rather than focusing on their grim situation, these men, highly trained, disciplined and rallied by a strong leader were mobilizing, organizing, and focusing on the matters within their control, most importantly, their attitudes.

This is a lesson for all of us as we slog through the backside of a long recession, bad headlines, and nasty political season. It's easy to get caught up in the negativity and have it affect our outlook, attitude and even the relationships with those we care about but the challenge is always to focus on what we can control and let the rest take care of itself, because it will whether we worry about it or not.

It seems that Collin has taken the reigns from his cousin as the family fishing king. Last weekend, I thought I'd woken up before the rooster but as I sat down at the computer for my morning paperwork ritual, Collin came bursting in from the backyard. It was 6:30 am and he'd already been fishing on the neighbor's pier for nearly an hour. He'd been "killing it" and got me to come out with him to join in the fun. When all was said and done, he'd landed two beautiful Redfish… one 24 and the other 21 ½ inches. To top it off, that night, oldest son Alex did the grilling and we dined on a meal fit for the restaurant crowd. With Collin doing the catching, Alex doing the cooking, pretty soon I'm just going to be sitting in my rocking chair doing crosswords and talking about my colon.

October 2010

They say one man's trash is another man's treasure and Craig's List provides a wonderful forum to unite the two. It's amazing what you can sell on the site...I didn't think it would be hard to unload our old rowboat and used kayak, but it only took a few hours to get a hit on our used smoker grill as well. Seeing my success, Collin decided to get in on the action. He's long over his skateboard phase and had a bunch of old boards, helmets, wheels and miscellaneous parts that he decided to sell. He did a nice job laying them out, taking pictures and writing up the ad but I would have never thought anyone would offer money for this junk that's been scattered around my garage for years. There I go thinking again. He got several calls and we met a potential buyer in the Walmart parking lot where Collin closed the sale and earned some sweet moolah. I'm still trying to sell him on the Air Force Academy but if that doesn't pan out, I see Business School in the cards.

With the local economy still a bit in the dumps, it took a bit longer for my motorcycle but when I finally got the price right, a buyer drove in from Hattiesburg, Mississippi. It was bittersweet watching a stranger drive away on my Harley of the past four years but it was fun while it lasted, and since Kathleen had nothing to do with it and didn't let the boys near either, it was too much of a selfish pleasure. I've got to say that it did make up a sizable part of my machismo so to compensate, I've decided to grow a moustache, start smoking, and wear more denim.

It's nothing I've done consciously but over the years my practice has gravitated to an interesting niche...I have a statistically significant percentage of single women both widowed and divorced. I recently met with a woman referred from an existing client, both of this demographic. She was in her early 50's and recently widowed with a school age son. Tragically, her husband died after a battle with cancer and unfortunately, he had no life insurance. After reviewing her situation, she's going to be ok but it will be very tight. Please, please, please don't be in that position. If you have people who rely on your income and who's lifestyle would suffer if you were to suddenly depart, please have a sufficient term life insurance policy in place. It's called term because it's good for a period of time (20 years, 10 years, etc.) after which it's over. The term should match the need of your income... until your kids are on their own, your debts (mortgage, etc.) are paid off, or your retirement is funded. Term life insurance is very cheap because in most cases it is never paid, but in the cases that it is, it can mean the difference between your loved ones moving on or drastically moving down.

Time marches on...in many cases, much more quickly than we realize. I had a Twilight Zone like trip down memory lane last month at the Chamber of Commerce's

Military Affairs Committee luncheon. We meet monthly to hear from representatives from the major military bases who give us the scoop on the latest happenings. I have a huge soft spot in my heart for our service members partly because of the sacrifice that they make on a daily basis to protect our freedoms and also because of the memories it evokes of my 10 years in the Navy. Two reps from the Navy's Whiting Field (the Navy's most busy airfield) were book ends to my career. Retired Commander Bob Asmus was a department head at my first operational helicopter squadron at Barber's Point Hawaii, where I, as a young Officer and pilot was responsible for a good amount of his now silver hair. The current Base XO, was a flight student of mine back in the twilight of my career when I returned to my roots in the mid 90's. Since I taught and flew formation and low-level tactical navigation, he is no doubt responsible for a few of my silver hairs as well. What goes around comes around.

November 2010

"Advice is like snow; the softer it falls, the longer it dwells upon, and the deeper it sinks into, the mind."

Samuel Taylor Coleridge

Alex recently hit the first big milestone in a teenager's life. He's now packing his Learner's Permit. In his typical first-born, type-A fashion, he spent the weekend before his 15th birthday cramming for and passing the online pre-test in preparation for the real thing scheduled for the morning of his birthday. The test itself was pretty uneventful, Alex got the cherished ID card and as a reward for his diligence, I gave him the opportunity to take the wheel of my truck, for the first time officially and drive us to Gulf Breeze High School about 3 miles down the road. He really impressed me when he piped that mom didn't want him driving on Hwy 98 during the morning rush hour. Having spent three years as a helicopter flight instructor with young students planning my death every day, I told him not to worry, I'm ok. Once again, my young conservative first born displayed judgement beyond his years and took a pass on the offer. He insists that a career in engineering is in the cards but I see hedge fund manager.

The winds of time have been blowing a gale and for the past dozen years we've been holding on for dear life. Early in the month, Kathleen and I attended Alex's High School Open House and got to experience a-day-in-the-life of our freshman student. We trudged through the halls of the school and spent about 5 minutes in each of his classes, meeting his teachers and getting a thumbnail presentation of the curriculum. It was a lot of fun and brought back tons of memories (mostly painful for me) but the most telling part of the evening was looking at the other parents our age under the harsh fluorescent lights of a 30-year-old high school after a hard day's work. Who were all these tired middle-aged people? They looked vaguely like the folks we used to see…wasn't it just yesterday, when we picked our children up from Little Lambs pre-school.

Jon's passion

My folks

Best Day Ever!

Jon's Childhood Home

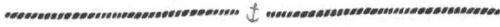

2011

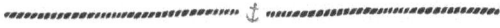

January 2011

"Don't be afraid to take a big step if one is indicated. You can't cross a chasm in two small jumps."

David Lloyd George

It's 5 months before Mothers' Day but here's an early shout out to the most under-appreciated of the parental units. Recently, Kathleen went directly to a Christmas party from work leaving me with the regular mom duties. Holy cow... it was non-stop. I made it home in time to take Collin to the store, go to the bank and a Walmart trip. No sooner than I walked in the door did Alex need to go to Walmart. We made it home and I prepared dinner during which Alex spilled his glass of milk. After dinner, I drove them to basketball practice, came home to remop the floor, and do a load of laundry before getting in a workout. Ay Caramba, I'm exhausted just writing about it! If your household presently contains a momma, how about giving her a big hug for no reason at all.

For the past decade or so, Kathleen's family has had a traditional dinner at her mom's (Annie) house, usually the night after Christmas. We typically have about 20 or so turn out for a casual dinner followed by the entertainment of watching all the cousins' open presents. To keep the adults engaged, Annie will always find a gift for her sons-in-law that involve some kind of flying projectile. Past years have brought mini marshmallow guns and rubber band shooters but this year's find was truly one-of-a-kind. In a bizarre tribute to the scariest scene from the Wizard of Oz, we spent the latter part of the evening hurling flying monkeys across the room at each other. The arms of these cute little stuffed creatures were attached by surgical tubing so they were their own little slingshots and as they flew by, they emitted an incredibly annoying screeching sound similar to the Geico commercial's "little piggy". Of course, my kids ended up bringing three of these horrid things home and spent the next week taunting their way-too-tolerant dad with the screeching until they learned an important lesson on "breaking points" and the creatures met a nasty fate on New Year's Eve...I hope yours was more relaxing!

February 2011

"If you don't know where you are going, you might wind up someplace else."

Yogi Berra

I received an email from the mom of one of Collin's buddies who volunteers at his school. They are looking for parents to come in and talk to the kids during their Career Class, giving them some insight into various careers out there in the world. I told her I'd love to come on in but when I let Collin in on the idea, he nearly begged me not to. In his words, "my friends already think you're weird, I don't want them to know it!" Nice kid but of course that sealed the deal...I'll let you know how the day went in a future newsletter.

Kathleen got some reinforcement that it's not just her husband that needs detailed instructions and doesn't make inferences well...it's the entire male species. Saturday, before setting off to Pilates class, she asked Collin to please put the clothes into the dryer before he leaves for baseball practice. Always the obedient son, he did as mom asked but when she returned from her workout, she discovered a dryer full of wet, clammy clothes. It turns out, she never told him to turn the dryer on (sounds like a Seinfeld episode). When Kathleen shared the story with a friend, said friend said that her retired big shot corporate executive did the same thing not so long ago. Now I know a sample size of three is pretty small to make the sweeping conclusion of the paragraph's beginning but I bet if we carried it out to this reading audience, we'd get similar results.

Alex, whose adventures in driving have passed the six-month mark, recently told me about a friend of his who is getting a 2006 BMW as her first car...you've got to love Gulf Breeze High...it's like an east coast "Beverly Hills 90210". I told him that he'd hate it if I did similar, to which he strenuously disagreed. Alex has some money in a fund that he's been contributing to over the past 5 years with birthday money and money from good report cards. After getting pretty hammered in the stock market's dumping of 2008/09, it's made it back up to the mid $3,000 level which should be enough to get an adequate first ride for the eager young lad. The other condition though, is to be employed since dad won't be throwing out gas money or cash for the upgraded stereo, so Alex is already getting his resume worked up and has his eye on the Kentucky Fried Chicken up the road. Time will tell which child learns more from his first car experience but I'm hoping our son's lesson will help sow the seeds of fiscal responsibility and delayed gratification.

March 2011

Spending the day with an eighth grade Career Class, I got a glimpse of the future, and it looked pretty promising. If things work as hoped, I met a future plastic surgeon, an architect, a veterinarian, an auto mechanic, a dentist, a musician, and a history professor. Most were going to college, several starting out in the military and a couple jumping into the family business. As eighth graders, these kids came in all shapes and sizes, most were firmly into what my niece describes as the "sea monster" stage where their bodies are not quite sure if they are kids or adults and they look like they could live quite comfortably on the Island of Dr. Moreau. It was truly a whirlwind of a day and the highlight of my week for sure since I am now well into my crusty old, "kids these days..." years and to see what is hopefully a cross-section of the future of this country with solid goals, dreams and aspirations made me think there just might be some hope for the future of my social security payments. You know what they say about payback and mine to son Collin came during my short power-point presentation in which every 3rd slide was a baby picture of my #2 son!

I've found there is no such thing as a "normal" family. That said, my own has more than its share of dysfunction (a friend told me that her family puts the "fun" in dysfunction). Personally, my dad and I share a history of long periods of silence, the longest being about 12 years which I broke last year when I called on his birthday. Not surprisingly, we had a nice chat having quite a bit of catching up to do, with the time lapse softening up whatever it was that caused the discourse in the first place. I went in for a repeat last month, giving the old man a ring on his 77th and once again it felt good. Life is short and I know it's none of my business, but if there's someone out there that you haven't reached out to in way too long, and if you would truly have regrets to read their obituary not having the opportunity to try "one more time," what do you have to lose?

As our kids grow older, the jokes and pranks get more involved which we saw firsthand waking up one recent Sunday morning to our first TP'ing. For those unfamiliar, a TP'ing is when a bunch of hooligans get together and under cover of darkness, hurl rolls of toilet paper throughout the yard of an unsuspecting victim. It is most dramatic when said victim has a yard full of trees (the taller the better!) for this TP to drape like garland on a Christmas tree. Ours was a sophomoric bunch with only one roll strewn across the front lawn, completely missing the prime old oak trees. The funny thing is that these days, kids actually do it to their friends which made me ask my boys which of their buddies were responsible. High-schooler Alex said it was definitely not his buddies because if it were, we would have had 500 rolls hanging on our trees and the same number of plastic forks and knives stuck in the lawn...a new and particularly egregious prank since cleanup requires the homeowner to bend down and pick up each utensil individually, good exercise for sure but not one you'll forget in the near term. To date, we still don't know who was responsible, but we are ever vigilant.

May 2011

"Don't believe the world owes you a living; the world owes you nothing - it was here first."

Robert Jones Burdette

I came home for a late lunch and was startled when Collin appeared from around the corner. Our normally upbeat chatterbox of a teenager was unusually forlorn with his head down and silent. When I asked him what was up, he put his head in his hands and started to cry. This just doesn't happen so I walked around the counter, gave him a hug and told him he could tell me when he was ready. In the ensuing moments, I went through a list of possible reasons for our son's condition.... wrong-place-at-the-wrong-time situation with something illegal; a fight in the hallway; a tragic medical diagnosis of a friend or teacher? In my mind, I flashed back about 35 years, and the list of possibilities was pretty scary. When he finally composed himself enough to share, it turned out that while on the bus on the way to a field trip, he was caught using his cellphone and had to go see the dean the next day which most likely would result in a "referral," his first blemish on an otherwise squeaky-clean middle school record. Bless his heart, I told him I was happy that he was so upset but it probably wouldn't have too big an impact on his long-term future goals and dreams. I guess our kids aren't so bad…at least so far.

June 2011

"There is only one way to happiness and that is to cease worrying about things which are beyond the power of our will."

Epictetus

Born into slavery in the year 55 AD, this month's quote-smith eventually earned his freedom and began to teach philosophy, his passion. Nearly two thousand years later, Admiral James Stockdale would credit Epictetus with helping him endure seven and a half years in a North Vietnamese military prison—including torture—and four years in solitary confinement. The flip side of the quote is that much of our life is in our hands and we are the only true masters of our destiny. Don't like your job, take the initiative to acquire the skills needed for that career of your dreams. Unhappy with how you look in a bathing suit, join the YMCA. From the young man born without a right leg who went on to win the NCAA National wrestling championship, to the concert pianist who was born blind and severely autistic, we can find examples every day of those who refused to become victims of their circumstances and rose to heights never imagined, by the sheer power of their will, determination, and unrelenting efforts.

July 2011

,,

"We should never despair, our Situation before has been unpromising and has changed for the better, so I trust, it will again. If new difficulties arise, we must only put forth New Exertions and proportion our Efforts to the exigency of the times."

George Washington.

Who'd have thunk it? Collin graduated the 8th grade. Even more incredible to fathom, in just eight years, Kathleen and I will be empty nesters with a pair of college grads off the payroll and contributing to society. I've been doing my best to create an environment where our kids would rather hop a freight train across the country than come back home after graduating so I'm counting on that eight-year thing to stick. Middle school has sure changed since I was there back in the days of chalk and knuckle-wrappings. You can definitely tell the kids that eat the organic poultry versus the majority of those munching on the steroid-enhanced Walmart brand. The latter produce 14-year-old girls who are 6'2" and look like they could teach eighth grade and boys that could be starting lineman at Auburn except for the Justin Bieber hairdos. We hit another

Collin milestone last night...his first shave. He could have just as easily used tweezers but instead, got mom to buy him a razor, so we hit the shaving cream and he got busy on his boy-stache. When I shared the news with my brother, he said he didn't shave until Army Basic Training and only because they made him. Gotta be the Walmart chicken which is okay because we need this generation to be strong enough to work hard and keep paying our social security.

August 2011

If you're like me, when you hear the title Explosive Ordnance Disposal (EOD) technician you think of the movie "Hurt Locker" and wonder who would be crazy enough to volunteer for such duty. Well, I was honored to meet the family of Air Force Technical Sergeant Daniel "P Nut" Douville, who was on his second tour in Afghanistan when he made the ultimate sacrifice. After successfully disarming a suspicious looking object that turned out to be an IED, he triggered a second hidden device on his way back to the safe area. It was awe inspiring to hear from members of his team...from young Airmen under his wing, to his boy-faced Captain who looked like Doogie Howser with muscles, and finally his Colonel who praised the Sergeant's unwavering commitment to his troops and country and read the citation for his Bronze Star Medal (with valor and one oak leaf cluster).

The most stirring testament came from his wife and mother of their three beautiful children. A woman of amazing faith, she explained that she finds her strength in knowing that he is watching over the family and if she were to cry, she'd hear his voice and the line that he often used with their children, "your tears do not impress me…if you're not happy with the way things are going, change them." She recalled the scene where the men in uniform were at her door bringing the news of her husband's "untimely" death. She quickly corrected them saying that it was "exactly" his time and she would not second guess God on the matter. The strength, character and faith of our men and women in uniform and the families that support them is something that never ceases to inspire and amaze me.

From faith to the innocence, wonder and promise of children. Oliver is the son of my wife's best-friend Liz and her husband George. They are raising four great kids and just shipped off their eldest to his first year at the University of Florida (apologies to the Seminoles out there) In school, when asked to write, "what do you see when you look inside yourself?" Oliver, just ten years old came up with this. "When I look in the mirror, I see someone unique to everyone else; someone who will change the world, someone who will be remembered. I look at the mirror at a glance and see a bright future. I do not see a person another would envy, but still a great person. I see myself." When I read that little essay, I see a boy who is going to be a positive influence on so many around him in ways he won't even know and I can only hope there are lots of other young men and woman out there that have a similar view of the world and their place in it.

September 2011

Life is all about balance. Kathleen, her sister Carrie, and their mom Annie, made a road-trip to Orlando for a long weekend to celebrate niece Kate's birthday. The boys and I spent three days without the balancing influence of estrogen in the house. I am an introvert and workaholic, but being a family man forces me to expand on my otherwise natural tendencies. Our boys, as typical high school teenagers, don't have much use for dad unless it involves opening the wallet or a lift somewhere. But they surprised me this weekend. First, Alex decided to step up to take care of the laundry so momma didn't return to an overflowing hamper. And Collin, who'd ticked me off earlier on "respect" issues, apologized sincerely and admitted his friends aren't as enlightened as he on the honor thy father and mother commandment. I felt a bit like Brian Keith on the classic 60's show "A Family Affair" but with my boys stepping up their game, I didn't need Mr. French. Of course, having Kathleen is the best gift of all and one I always appreciate even more in her absence.

October 2011

Collin has been bitten by the surfing bug in a huge way. When Tropical Storm Irene approached the Louisiana coastline, it was far enough away that the weather here was gorgeous. It was close enough that the waves were "epic" and Collin convinced us to let him go surf with a large group of friends since one of the mom's would be there the whole time. What I failed to take into account was how Collin's rugged individualism, when coupled with the awesome power of Mother Nature, might lead him to take things closer to the edge than we'd be comfortable with.

The scare began when Kathleen received a phone call at about 5 pm from the surf mom telling her that the rest of the boys had returned to shore but Collin and a buddy were still enjoying the rare "double overhead" event (surf speak for big waves). At 5:30 with still no sign of the two, Kathleen headed for the beach. At 6:00, the boys still AWOL, we now were getting quite concerned and the local police and lifeguards joined the search. As the sun set, we were now in panic mode and as I drove to the scene, I asked God out loud to please join the search party. A few minutes later, I got a call from eldest son Alex that Collin was at the pier and was greeted with a bear-hug from a mom who broke down upon seeing him. It turned out, the carefree young lad and his buddy decided to let the surf carry them down wind and when they finally exited the water, they were so far away that they needed to hop the trolley to return to the starting point. We had a thorough debriefing about responsibility, accountability and added grounding for good measure which will hopefully make the lesson stick for at least a few months.

Alex turns 16 this week and I just learned that my auto insurance will more than double as a result. I know these kids will pay off eventually, I guess I just need to consider them long-term investments. We did get a surprise from Alex over the past few weeks. Alex has always been the strong, silent type and I assumed that his interest in the "ladies" would take a back seat to studying and ESPN at least for the next several years. We were quite surprised when he asked if he could go out to the beach with a girl who had asked him and would be picking him up in her truck. I've got to say that as a dad, I was very proud of our first born and the fact that an upper-class-woman had an interest. I know it's a double-standard and if the tables were turned and Alex had been born Alexis, this thing would be squashed before it began. It turned out they skipped the beach and instead, went out to dinner, meeting her folks at a local restaurant. I was even more impressed with the new venue, given the added pressure of having to perform in front of his new friend's dad on their first "date". All went predictably well; Alex passed muster with dad and has entered a new realm from which there is no return.

December 2011

> *"Happiness does not depend on what happens outside of you but on what happens inside of you. It is measured by the spirit with which you meet the problems of life."*
>
> Harold B. Lee

Keep the above quote in mind when you read about Bob Bell on the last page of this missive. I've written of my cousin-in-law in the past and since the last update, he is working as an Associate Professor at his Alma Mater, St John's. Recently, while grading papers on the subject of individual rights, specifically euthanasia, one of his students made what he thought was a compelling case. "What about the humiliation one might suffer from being in a wheelchair everywhere they go...If everything you ever loved to do, and enjoyed in life were taken away from you, you of course would want to end your life as well." Apparently, this student failed to notice that his professor was leading the class from a wheelchair where he's been for the past 22 years. More on that to follow.

Kathleen and I just went over 18 years of wedded bliss. They say that couples start looking like each other after a while. If so, I can only hope that it's my form that starts to morph but, in any case, we had a funny thing happen as we opened the little tokens of affection we picked up for each other to celebrate the day. As I opened my card, I broke into a smile when I saw that she picked the same card for me that I chose for her...on different days and at different places. And it wasn't one of those mushy ones with flowering fields and silhouettes, but one showing an older couple sitting comfortably beside each on a pair of weathered Adirondack chairs and watching a beautiful sunset from a peaceful dock. The wife makes a sniffing sound and asks, "Burrito for lunch?" to which the husband causally replies, "Broccoli." You open the card to the age-old reflection that Loves means never having to say, "Excuse me." Our marriage, like anything worth a damn, hasn't been all "roses" but it hasn't been all broccoli either and I can't imagine spending the next 18 with anyone else.

Athletics

Silliness

Intro
to the
Military

Life is good

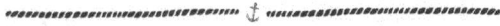

2012

January 2012

"The greatest mistake you can make in life is to continually fear you will make one."

Elbert Hubbard

My sister-in-law Joanie used to send her boys out the door with the instructions, "take risks, get dirty, make mistakes" and so far, it's worked. They're still young but Benjamin, Noah and Peter are on their way to becoming wonderfully caring and highly productive caretakers of this planet. As for this month's quote-smith, Mr. Hubbard was quite a character. According to Wikipedia, Bertie, as his family called him, was an American author, artist and publisher. He began his adulthood as a self- proclaimed anarchist and socialist but later evolved as an ardent defender of "free enterprise and American know-how", credited with the quote "Prison is a Socialist's Paradise, where equality prevails, everything is supplied and competition is eliminated." Three years after penning a moving commentary on the death of Ida Strauss, a passenger onboard the Titanic who refused a spot on a lifeboat, choosing instead to remain with her husband, he and his wife met a similar fate onboard the Lusitania after it was struck by a torpedo from a German submarine.

February 2012

As always, a carefully considered long-term strategy is the key which brings us to this month's quote-smith. Given the volatility of the past three years…heck, the past ten years, a well thought out, purpose driven financial plan has never been more important. That said, using the inimitable cowboy's quote as a metaphor, a financial plan is a living document that needs to be dusted off regularly to account for changes in your life as well and the environment in which we live.

I often brag that Alex, our firstborn son, is a 45-year-old trapped in a 16-year old's body. Though we're intellectually about the same age, my neuroses are thankfully completely absent from the young lad's persona. He does, however, possess the inner drive that wakes me up regularly at 2:00 am worrying about what I need to get done in the upcoming 24 hours and I noted it while he was studying one night last month. It turns out that the 85% he got on a recent math test dropped his overall grade to a low A and the upcoming test was crucial to keep him in his comfort zone. Not to worry...his methodical, anxiety-free studying payed off and the 100% on the next exam sealed a 4.0 for semester two of his sophomore year of High School. Whose genes created this boy?

It's basketball season and I've got to say that of all the spectator sports that our sons have forced upon us, roundball is the most exciting for us. Both boys have played pretty much everything, and from a selfish standpoint (it is all about us, right?!), some sports have been pretty agonizing from a fan's perspective. But in basketball, Collin has found his place. The lad has always been a scrappy one, no doubt a case of little brother syndrome, but his growth spurt a couple years back, and his Keith Richards physique have really given him an edge. Top it off with this year's excellent team and solid coaching and we've had a heck of a season with a couple buzzer-beating half court shots to boot.

March 2012

There is something cleansing about getting back to your roots and so it was recently on a crisp and clear Saturday morning when we found ourselves in the beautiful synagogue of Temple Beth-El, honored to be a part of Ansley Segal's Bat Mitzvah ceremony. The daughter of good friends Dr. Frank and Julie Segal, Ansley's "Coming of Age" is a sacred ceremony performed when a Jewish child reaches the age of thirteen and indicates a willingness to accept responsibility in personal, family, community and religious matters taking an important step towards maturity. Ansley did a wonderful job reading the day's portion of the Torah, the most sacred of the Five Books of Moses, handwritten in Hebrew on parchment and rolled onto two scrolls. It had been eons since I was in her place but I did my best to follow along as she read and the memories came flooding back…the "pain" washed away by the decades passed! I was raised a Jew in the Northeast, both of my parents were first generation American born offspring of Eastern European immigrants (Russia in my dad's case, Hungary my mom's).

After college, I joined the Navy and on my second trip through Pensacola, met and married my soulmate Kathleen, who'd been raised Catholic. After our boys were born, we chose a religious tie-breaker and began attending a Methodist church around the corner from our house. It's all the same God and has worked for us although there's always been a little guilt, it's a Jewish thing. That is until I read a piece on Judaism from the Bat Mitzvah program. It read, "Judaism does not teach that it is the only way to universal truth. We do not believe that in the End of Days all peoples will flow to us and we will be one. Harmony, not conformity, is our goal. Pluralism, not universalism, is our message. Let each people walk in the love of God." Hallelujah. Now that I've covered religion, let's move on to sex and politics.

Kathleen and I were treated to a night of classic American pop culture a couple of weeks back when we caught a live performance of legendary funny man, Jerry Seinfeld. The man whose eponymous TV show about nothing which gave us timeless lexicon like, "yadda, yadda, yadda", "re-gifting", "sponge-worthy", and "Festivus", put on a hilarious performance at the warm and cozy Saenger Theater in Pensacola. In classic Seinfeld fashion, he never once talked about politics, current events, or anything of any real significance…his act is all about the trivial commonalities we share as human beings. On relationships he observes, "Marriage is like being in the Lightning Round of a game-show all the time. I'll take, "five-minute conversations we had two years ago at 3 in the morning for one hundred!" On the subject of life he waxes, "they say that life is short…

it's actually way too long. Old people are sitting on cruise ships doing crossword puzzles just trying to finish the damn thing up...it's exhausting!" On food, "Everywhere we go people always tell us that there is this restaurant that we have to go to because the food is great. I don't even like that. You know what I want...not bad." He was hilarious and if he makes it back or visits a town near you, it's worth the trip.

April 2012

As I type this Saturday morning, our 16-year-old son Alex is busy getting ready for the first day of his first job. As a dad, I really don't think I could be any prouder as this is the first step to "mission accomplished" in my view, of being a parent. I've long held that once a couple makes the commitment to bringing another little creature to this world, the number one mission of their ever-changed lives is to prepare the kid with the requisite skills to leave the nest and hopefully make a positive contribution to the planet. Work ethic, in my humble opinion, is one of the most important values of humanity and this morning is the culmination of 16 plus years of hammering that into our first-born son. As Alex heads to the Hilton at Pensacola Beach for his first day's duties as "towel-boy", beware the scofflaws who'd misbehave or abscond with hotel property. There's a new sheriff in town!

Collin, on the other hand, is a bit more of a risk-taker. He also recognizes the social and economic importance of employment but he's a bit less of a company man and a bit more entrepreneurial. His first step into the working world is a leap into small business, setting up a lawn mowing enterprise - carrying on a family tradition begun by his old man nearly 40 years back. Like all new ventures, it has modest beginnings. His current client list is just two very satisfied customers (one being his grandmother) but I have no doubt that our young entrepreneur will soon be a big player in his niche market, the Bay Colony subdivision of Tiger Point.

May 2012

As promised, with employment secured, we began in earnest, the search for Alex's first car. Of course, Alex had begun his online research months prior and every night he'd come across potential candidates while scrolling through the local Craig's Listings. Both our boys have been saving for this goal for about six years in their "investment". Said investment was a mutual fund that I initially seeded and added to when either an honor roll report card was produced or when, on their own volition, they chose to add birthday, lawn mowing, or miscellaneous funds of their own. Like the rest of us, the boys went through the financial mess of 2008-09 and their account took a considerable hit. But like good investors, they kept at it (as if they had a choice) and Alex now had enough put away to buy his first ride. After vetting several potential candidates, he ultimately decided to go with a 2002 Jeep Liberty that he bought from one of Kathleen's co-workers. I've got to say he looks pretty good behind the wheel and I think that he's proud that his ownership is a result of six years of delayed gratification...a great lesson for a kid (or grown-up) of any age. The best part is that he didn't take after his pop who turned his first car into a mangled mess of twisted metal and cracked Bondo after about a day and a half.

June 2012

> *"The significant problems we face cannot be solved at the same level of thinking we were at when we created them."*
>
> Albert Einstein

On a much happier note, I recently took a road trip down to Orlando for the Raymond James National Conference. It was a first-class event, as always, and since driving cross-country in college, I've loved hitting the road. Add to that, an iPhone app called Spotify that allows you access nearly every song, by every artist ever published and I was almost sad to get to the destination. A cool feature of the app is that as you enjoy a song, it suggests other similar songs and artists that you might like which leads you on an endless journey through musical nirvana. A couple hours into the drive, I landed on Harry Chapin's "Cats in the Cradle" … the chart topper from 1974 about a young boy who longs to "hang out" with his dad, but at every request, his dad brushes him off…he's too busy right now but maybe later. The child, magical as kids are, is undeterred and instead of being put off, idolizes his pop and vows to be just like him. The end of the story finds the son, all grown up with kids of his own, coming full circle and when his elderly father calls to see about a get together, his son turns the table and dad realizes as he hangs up the phone, "my boy is just like me." I more than mist up every time I hear that damn song and I'm getting "damp" just writing about it because it hits home just a bit.

Keeping with that theme, the end of my trip down south was highlighted by a rendezvous with my folks. We met at a neat riverfront restaurant down in Tampa, a point midway from their home in Sarasota and my conference in Orlando because, not unlike the song above, I had to get back to Pensacola the next day for several appointments. I hadn't seen my dad in over 15 years so the hour or so we spent sharing a meal was pretty special. He is a man of few words so I did most of the talking and spent the majority of the time on the subject of my boys and the trials and tribulations of teaching them how to become men. I know that he enjoyed hearing my tales…he even said such and as I write this, I think that on his drive back home, he might have reflected "my boy is just like me." I hope it made him happy.

July 2012

"Life is a tragedy when seen in close-up, but a comedy in long-shot."

Charlie Chaplin

It's different this time...the great recession, gridlock in Washington, the 1%, the decline of Europe, global warming...from what we read and see on the news, it almost makes you hope the Mayans got it right. But if we step back a minute and take a trip through history, we'll see that Charlie Chaplin called it with his quote above. It always seems worse than it is and times always seem tougher than they've ever been...we are creatures of immediacy and we live in the present. Unless we take the time to read about days gone by, we have nothing with which to compare our present challenges so we view them against a fantasy world where everything goes our way, we have unlimited resources, and we all just get along...it worked for Adam and Eve in the short run but we know how that turned out.

August 2012

> *"The inherent vice of capitalism is the unequal sharing of blessings; the inherent virtue of socialism is the equal sharing of miseries."*
>
> Winston Churchill

Isn't election year politics fun? We're getting quite an earful on what's fair, who built what, and who pays taxes and who doesn't. Regardless of the side of the aisle you sit, it should be clear that the irascible Winston Churchill had it right when he addressed the House of Commons in October of 1945. Capitalism, like any system, has its flaws but it is the only system that incentivizes those who take risks. Steve Jobs could not have existed in Cuba, Russia or China…he'd have ended up in prison at best. And those nations that have resisted are moving closer and closer to the American brand of capitalism because it's led to the creation of the greatest economy in the history of economies. I'm confident that whomever is sworn into office next January, life will go on and free-market based capitalism will continue to bring innovation that we can't even imagine, improving the quality of life for all along the way.

A few weeks back, Alex told me he'd had the worst dream. He said it was so real that when he woke up, he was shaking and had that awful feeling of dread until he came back to the conscious world and realized his vision was just that. His dream, he told me, was that we were out boating and I was in the water when Uncle Boo who was at the wheel, accidentally ran me over killing me on the spot. Hearing this, I've got to say that I was taken back on two counts. First, that my eldest son was troubled by the occasional nightmare, and one so horrible at that. Second, that it affected him the way it did. When I was a 16 ½ year old, there was probably a time or two that a dream like that wouldn't have made me so upset, so it was nice to hear from my first born that his preferred state for his grouchy old man is alive.

Collin recently entered the driving scene and I've got to say it's causing ME some nightmares. Those that have followed our sons know that while Alex is the conservative, Alex Keaton type, Collin is our free-spirit. That same care-free, whimsical way has carried over to his driving and all I can say is YIKES! The good news is that I get to re-live some of my adrenaline-charged days as a helicopter flight instructor while I sit in the passenger seat and coach him on his "scan", turn signal etiquette and the finer points of lane-changes. I know that it's just a matter of getting that windshield time but I'm thinking that Collin's car fund might just turn into a college fund and that the best transportation option for him may just be providing gas money to one of his buddies with a car.

We have the best neighbors in the world. Jorge and Gina moved next door about 10 years ago after retiring from a pair of high powered and high stress jobs in the Big Apple.

Jorge was born in Argentina and he and Gina have lived in Panama and travelled all around the globe during their 30-year marriage. As such, they have friends from all over the place and given their good-nature, their house sometimes takes the nature of a bed and breakfast. They currently have some old friends from Argentina over for about 10 days and Collin got a little taste of South American culture last weekend. Collin is our fisherman and enjoys spending time on the Jorge's dock doing his best to keep the speckled trout and redfish population under control. Late last Saturday afternoon, while plying his trade, Collin looked up to see a young Argentine woman of 16 coming up to meet him and introduce herself. To Collin's surprise, in Argentina, rather than extending a right hand to introduce yourself, the customary greeting is to lean in and kiss both cheeks of the person you're greeting. Collin is 15 and on the front end of figuring this whole "girl thing" out so when this strange girl made the move, he jumped as if a combination of Freddy Kruger and Jason from the Halloween movies jumped out of the shadows. The poor girl was so embarrassed but it all ended well.

September 2012

"Work keeps at bay three great evils: boredom, vice, and need."

Voltaire

I knew the day would come. While out to dinner with friends, I asked Theresa if I could borrow her reading glasses. It was a bit dark in the restaurant and the menu's font was one of those squiggly, artsy types so I figured I'd give her cheaters right back as they wouldn't help given the conditions. WOW...I now understand what Kathleen felt like when she got her first pair of blue "cat's eye" specs as a little girl. She said that for the first time she saw that trees had "individual" leaves and the real world didn't look like a LeRoy Neiman painting. Okay it wasn't that dramatic but I knew that I'd entered a place from which there was no return. I AM my father...at least in looks, while I'm reading.

Last month, Alex had his first automobile mishap. Well, when it rains, it pours. He found out the very next day that week would be his last and his newly indebted state ($1,000 loan from dad to get the car fixed) was accompanied by unemployment. It was a timely lesson, given the economy and slow recovery from the Great Recession. Alex learned that it's not much fun being a debtor when the debt collector lives so close, so out of necessity, he changed his condition. Alex's new gig is at Taco Bell in Gulf Breeze and he's jumped in with both feet. It is quite a change from the quiet life of a hotel towel boy and he likes the fast-pace of fast food where he's racking up some hours working 5 days a week, with a full high school course-load and Cross-Country practice. Possibly the best part of the experience is a cultural one. For the non-locals, our Gulf Breeze High School is about as non-diverse as they come...kind of a redneck version of Beverly Hills 90210. At Taco Bell, Alex is one of only two Caucasians with the majority of employees being African American, including his boss who has taken him under her wing. Alex is loving the experience and will get so much more from it than the minimum wage he's earning.

October 2012

—————————————————————————————

Back in the early 60's, Honda introduced the slogan, "You Meet the Nicest People on a Honda." The advertising campaign showed housewives, young couples and otherwise respectable folks experiencing the joys of motorcycle ownership. A few weeks back, Kathleen and I joined our friends Chuck and Brenda at an event that made me think of that iconic slogan. A transplanted Yankee from Massachusetts, I would have never thought it, but you meet the nicest people at a gun show. Last month I told you that Kathleen had taken the handgun safety course and we were now ready to make a purchase. We aren't stocking canned food, buying gold and water purification tablets in preparation for the zombie apocalypse...no offense to my friends out there who are (you might get the last laugh!) But after going to the shooting range with Uncle Boo last fall, we thought it would be a fun occasional winter time hobby and if the Mayans are right, we'd want to be prepared. After lots of looking and talking with nice folks at the show, we decided on a Taurus 357 revolver for the simplicity, cost of ammo (you can shoot cheap .38 rounds at the range and have .357 rounds for the zombies), and price. We've already been to the shooting range to test it out, had a great time and in a weird way, it was even a bit romantic.

You know it's not a good thing when you're on a first name basis with the local Auto Body Shop but that's where we find ourselves. After Kathleen's encounter with the drunk driver and Alex's inaugural fender-bender on the infamous Highway 98, Collin got into the action last month. Thank goodness, no one was hurt, but my goofball second born got a Physics lesson, testing the old Force equals Mass times Acceleration equation when he backed Aunt Debbie's golf cart, at full speed, into the side of my truck. It was an expensive lesson that took a big chunk out of his car fund (he's been saving for over 5 years) but I am pretty confident he will not repeat the mistake. Here's a quick shout out to Gulf Breeze's Bayside Collision who did a great job and saved me $600 by repairing versus replacing the quarter panel.

November 2012

"Creditors have better memories than debtors."

Ben Franklin

I often describe our eldest son Alex as a Vulcan…defined by Wikipedia as "an extraterrestrial humanoid species in the Star Trek universe who are noted for their attempt to live by reason and logic with no interference from emotion." He gave further proof last month when he called me at work and calmly asked if I might be able to get him from running practice and take him to the hospital, "I think I broke my finger". When he asked me to please hurry, I realized it might be serious. We met in the parking lot, Alex produced his shockingly twisted digit, and I was amazed by his demeanor. In his usual monotone, he calmy noted, "It's probably not broken because there's no swelling…probably just dislocated". He was right, of course, and the girls at the Urgent Care Clinic got a kick out of his condition, giving them something exciting to finish out their day. It all ended well and three weeks later all we have is a memory and a really cool picture for posterity's sake.

It's Movember, a global movement to raise awareness of men's health issues, specifically prostate and testicular cancer. For 30 days, men (and I imagine even some women!) let their freak flag fly by growing and cultivating their collective moustaches becoming walking, talking billboards for the movement. Why you ask, am I telling you this? Well, it turns out, I'm not just providing info, I'm a participant currently sporting an attempt at a goatee. Don't be scared, it's still me but I've got to say that I think people are taking me more seriously with this thing. To those moms whose children I made cry, I apologize.

December 2012

I'm back. After a two-year absence, I've returned to the motorcycle brotherhood and I can say with conviction that there's no place like home. Mentally, just like you're never an Ex-Marine, you never leave the brotherhood. I still found myself giving the biker wave to people on scooters while driving my truck. But this time it's not a Harley. I rode a Softtail Deluxe for 4 years and enjoyed the experience immensely…it made watching "Sons of Anarchy" even more compelling as I thought, "I could do that", except for the gun/drug-running, prostitution, prison, and murder stuff. For my ride this time, I chose a different but equally enigmatic steed. I'm the third owner of this beauty, a 96 BMW R1100RS, which just went over 95,000 miles, but these babies just get broken in at 100,000. The previous owner, a 66-year-old retired airline pilot, just got back from a 9,000-mile ride up to the Pacific Northwest. Now I just need to convince my "old lady" that there's no place like the truly open road and get her into the scene.

I have some huge news on the kid front. Collin, now 15, got his first job. To be fair, he had a pretty nice lawn mowing gig over the summer but once the grass stopped growing, welfare (allowance) was not going to allow him the lifestyle that he had come to enjoy. So, he is working where every kid ought to start out (in my opinion), at the bottom of the food chain in the food industry, as a restaurant dishwasher. He's taking care of business at one of our favorite local jaunts, "Papa Nalu's Aloha Grill" in the Tiger Point area. Paul and Deborah's hidden gem is tucked in on the end a strip mall. Paul took his years in the industry coupled with his Hawaiian heritage and opened a truly unique place that has stood the test of time in a difficult environment. The pressure is on though because I told Collin he will be very sorry if he does anything to make it uncomfortable for me and his mom to frequent the place. Yah, life is both hard and unfair.

Father's Day

Business Partners

Me and
my brothers

Love you

Christmas chaos
at Annie's

2013

January 2013

As a dad with a pair of sons, unquestionably one of life's greatest joys is watching your little snot-nosed boys turn into young men. Sure, they're smelly, hairy and take way too long in the shower, but when you see them solve problems, develop cogent opinions and enunciate them in a fairly articulate manner, it's pretty doggone cool. We've always been a practical family and we carry that trait into our gift-giving so during this holiday season, when looking at what to do for Alex, we thought why not set him up with some of the parts that he needed to get his car back to a more fully functional state. He agreed and got busy searching the internet for a driver's side door lock actuator and left passenger power window regulator for his 2002 Jeep that was suffering from a typical mid-life crisis. The parts came about a week later and we got busy. It wasn't easy for me but I held back and let the young man take charge. Watching him in action was a beautiful thing. He patiently tackled the task at hand with a thorough competence that foreshadowed a future as a successful engineer, his long-stated goal after college. The best part was watching his satisfaction when both jobs were complete and his car was once again, fully mission capable all by his own doing. Can you hear the Harry Chapin lyrics?

Christmas was extra special this year because we got to enjoy it with the newest addition to the family. Niece Kate and her husband Drew were in town from Orlando and with them, sweet baby James, their four-month-old son who still had that new baby smell. I'm not sure how manly it is but I have always loved babies, even my own. There's just something so magical and nothing more indicative of the existence of our creator...they just make my heart happy. And when you get the little things to smile and make that belly laugh...now if that could be turned into a pill, there is no doubt in my former military mind that it could cure asthma, the common cold, rudeness and quite possibly fix the national debt. All babies are wonderful but a dear friend of mine from the Philippines told me that when your niece or nephew has a baby, you're not a Great-Uncle, you're more a grandpa and holding baby James brought that home completely.

A couple weeks back, we made it up to the country where we joined our friends, Max and Theresa at the shooting range. Max is the only redneck metrosexual that I know. He can tear down an engine from an old Mustang on the same day that he hand-paints some antique furniture, arranges a flower setting, and when the sun sets, he'll prepare one of the best gourmet dinners you've ever had! He's a country boy from Alabama and retired Executive from the Pharmaceutical industry. He brought a couple of his pistols as well as an AK-47 that he'd picked up as a collector's piece. It was a lot of fun to shoot and I have some great pictures of Kathleen taking a turn. I know this has turned into a big political issue with the horrible tragedy in Newtown but I can honestly say that we have never met anyone but the nicest, most respectful and friendly folks at the range and the show where we purchased our firearm. How's that for an ending after talking about babies.

February 2013

Just when we thought our boys were all grown up, we got a humorous flashback to the old days. Collin has always been a bit nyctophobic; it comes with the whole sensitivity package. Alex on the other hand, devoid of most emotion, never let life after sunset bother him, nor much of anything for that matter. His one little personal kryptonite was watching scary movies. He wouldn't go as far as leaving the room because that would be admitting defeat. However, defeat didn't include watching from the safety of the backside of the couch with eyes closed and ears plugged. I thought he'd put this fear to bed (for the record there is no term for fear of scary movies, it's just called fear of scary movies!), until recently watching one such flick from our new subscription to Netflix. Just like the old days, when the exorcism scenes got particularly intense, Al turned back into a 7-year-old which was way more entertaining to me and Kathleen than the B movie we were tolerating.

March 2013

"The greatest danger in times of turbulence is not the turbulence; it is to act with yesterday's logic."

Peter Drucker

Women take notice. When you've been married for nearly twenty years, it gets tougher and tougher to find a unique gift for your sweetheart. Birthday, Anniversary, Mothers' Day, Christmas…Oh, the humanity! We men mean it when we tell you that you don't need to get us anything for Arbor Day, just having you is all the gift we need. So last month, when Valentine's Day reared its ugly head, I finally thought of something that I'd never presented before. We live in the woods and believe it or not, are not hooked up to the city sewer system, we have a septic tank. Before you get too grossed out, these things work great. Our soil is pretty much the white sand that makes up our beaches, an excellent filter and the drain field is the greenest part of the lawn. But with this system, you have to periodically get a pump out to keep things "running". Perfect timing, Happy Valentine's Day honey. Kathleen and I have a special relationship… I don't recommend this for the home viewers.

Collin has entered the brave new world that Alex journeyed to a year or two back...his first girlfriend. Like Alex, it was a good learning experience. Cost of living increase, the whole gift-giving dilemma from above, transportation issues and a new concern for personal grooming. Alas, like his brother, it was a short-lived affair...a good thing but as I told him during a debrief over ping pong, every time it gets a little easier and even more fun. Something I also saw for the first time in our second born son, a little bit of a study ethic. Collin is an excellent student like his brother, but unlike his brother, needs a little pressure to be at his best (like his father) When the deadline for his research paper finally began to blare like an air raid siren, I saw him pull his version of the college all-nighter to get the job done. Sunday night, the light was still on in his room as Kathleen and I hit the hay and the next morning, when I went to the kitchen for my coffee, the light once again peered from under his door. He did get a few hours of sleep in between and yes, I would rather see him take on the project in a less drastic fashion, but I was very impressed that he got the job done. The best part...it was an outstanding paper.

April 2013

> *"Any man who thinks he can be happy and prosperous by letting the government take care of him better take a closer look at the American Indian."*
>
> Henry Ford

Spring Break is history but we made some excellent memories. Channeling Horace Greeley, we went west for an epic ski trip. Three years of saving credit card miles got us the airfare; Vacation-Rentals-by-Owner (VRBO.com) found us a one-bedroom condo within walking distance to the slopes, Priceline and my pal William Shatner scored a full-size rental car for the price of a compact, and buying lift tickets in advance online saved us 30%. We chose Park City, Utah for its quaint old town shops that would give Kathleen an alternative if she decided 4 days of sliding down a frozen hill wasn't going to do it for her (Florida girl). Now I grew up in the Northeast and got my first official job at 14 to fund a budding skiing addiction. Alex and Collin, Southern boys by birth, have spent many hours strapped to a board towed behind a boat so for them, it was snowboarding which they've done a couple times over the past decade on trips to Vermont to visit my brother Jay and his family. The weather was beautiful, almost too warm on the first day but snow on day two took care of the conditions for the rest of the trip.

Skiing wise, the highlight for me and the boys came on our last day. The upper peaks of the mountain are surrounded by a series of "bowls", wide open snow-covered expanses above the tree-line accessible only by hiking. They're a majestic sight and rated double black diamond in difficulty making for some excellent bragging rights down the road. For fun, I suggested that we go for it as an awesome way to close out a great trip. I should have known that Collin would be in. No putting that cat back in the bag! To my surprise, Alex went along as well, the peer pressure a greater force than his sensibilities. So, after recharging our batteries at lunch, it was off to Jupiter Bowl. The hike itself was a challenge as we were at 10,000 ft. and our Sea-Level tuned lungs screamed after a few steps. At the top, I warned the boys before we pushed off. "Take your time and whatever you do, don't fall because there is nothing to stop you if you do." Well, we were off and doing great when wouldn't you know it, I took a header and slid for a football field or two before finding a lone tree to arrest my descent. Fifteen minutes later, at the bottom of the bowl, our adventure was complete. It wasn't exactly pretty, but we came, we saw, and we conquered.

It so happened St. Patrick's Day fell during the trip and wouldn't you know that downtown Park City had no shortage of appropriate venues to grab a bite and a few pints of Guinness. We chose Flanagan's on Main and were not disappointed. As you'd imagine, it was absolutely packed and just after we crammed our way in and got on the list, we were greeted by the cacophony of bagpipes. This was definitely the place to be but it was a bit much for our sheltered sons who decided to wait in the car until we were seated at a table. No worry for us, instant date night! The way-over-capacity crowd was a mixture of locals, the cast of Scorsese's "The Departed", ski tourists and most interesting (to me) a biker gang. Strangely out of place in a ski resort town in the winter, was a large group of the "Sons of Silence" motorcycle club, all dressed in their "colors" (leather jackets with club patches) that identified them as President, Vice President, several "old ladies" and even a "Prospect". It was like an episode of Sons of Anarchy. When I returned from the bar with refills, I found the VP standing next to Kathleen (who would obviously make a very attractive "old lady"). I chatted up the VP just enough not to get stabbed (they were called the Sons of Silence) and we moved on. Turned out the food was less than memorable, but the experience was worth it.

May 2013

«««««««««««««««««««««««««««««««««««««««

I don't have to tell you parents of teenagers that the milestone of hitting the big sixteen is anything but sweet from a financial standpoint. That pop in auto insurance rates is truly breathtaking and I guess it's just foreshadowing of what college is going to do to our cash flow in a couple of years. Our boys have had a "car fund" that I seeded about 7 years ago and added to when they either produced an honor roll report card or made deposits of their own. Each was invested in a mutual fund and though the crash of 2008 took a bite, Alex accumulated enough sweet moolah to buy his first used car about a year and a half ago. With Collin approaching the dreaded milestone, I told him that I didn't want another car on the insurance roster and instead, I'd give him liberal use of my truck and he could save his money for fun at college. You can imagine the arguments over fairness and the like which were answered by my standard "life ain't fair" quip. Enter Alex. In a surprising twist, he proposed that he and Collin both pay ½ of their insurance costs to keep my cash flow at the status quo. Who would have ever expected such a turn but how could I say no? Collin turns 16 on the 22nd of this month and I will be sure to tell you what kind of car to be on the lookout for in the near future. Where are my blood pressure meds?!

A couple weeks ago, I had the privilege of helping our niece Claren prepare for her first job interview. Claren is a sophomore at Gulf Breeze High School and a very squared-away young woman. She's been a competitive swimmer for years and currently swims for the High School. Naturally, her ideal job would be as a lifeguard at Pensacola Beach where she would be paid big bucks to hangout out at venue where people themselves pay big bucks and travel from around the world to enjoy. As you'd imagine, the competition is fierce and though Claren smoked the physical tests, the interview was uncharted territory and she wanted to nail it. No worries. I got online and put together 45 minutes of the most challenging questions I could dig up. I conducted the interview at my office and in character. It was huge fun (for me!) and with each difficult question, I watched Claren formulate an answer and knock it out of the park. Seeing a young person perform so well made my heart happy and gave me confidence that our nation's best days are still yet to come. By the way, Claren starts her job next week.

June 2013

So said the dark hero of AMC's Hell on Wheels as he rode off in search of his wife's killer in this post-Civil War drama that Kathleen and I found on Netflix. Despite the stock market's record run, many lament the decline of America and long for the good old days. My question to them is what good old days? The 50's had Happy Days and the Fonz but they also featured the Korean War, the Soviet's going nuclear, and a National Steel Workers strike. The 60's brought us JFK before he, his brother and Martin Luther King, Jr. were taken by assassins. The 70's brought us the personal computer, Apollo, and the first test tube baby but we also had Vietnam, a Presidential impeachment, and the Bee Gees. Truth is, there never was a "good old days", all times have highlights and lowlights because that is the nature of humanity. The good news is that we humans, particular those of us lucky enough to reside in a nation where our destiny is still, for the most part, in our own hands, tend to succeed when we figure out a way to provide a good or service that benefits others…that is the nature of an economy, and ours is still the model for the rest of the world. They don't call it the American Dream for nothing.

This year marks an epic milestone for folks like Kathleen and me. 2013 is the year that the majority of the High School class of 1981 turns 50. I've noticed my journey to "senior" status in several less significant ways over the years. First, when the Playboy centerfolds became my junior. Later, when Cadillac started using Led Zeppelin music in their ads, I suspected something was up. But that half-a-century mark is the clearest line in the sand that we're not getting any younger. But don't tell that to Kathleen's childhood BFF, Liz. We had the pleasure of attending her coming of age party thrown by husband George that featured local band DLP who became a literal "garage band" for the night, rocking out in the carport. DLP, which stands for doctors, lawyers and politicians (most of whom have already travelled 50 times around the sun) rocked the place for a solid couple hours and birthday girl Liz's non-stop dancing proved that 50 is most certainly the new 30.

Kathleen and I had an excellent date night a few weeks back. We took the ride into the big city of Pensacola to enjoy "Gallery Night". What used to be just a night that the local art galleries opened their doors for a little open house and hors d'oeuvres has evolved into a regular downtown festival with live bands, restaurants, and if you time it right, a fireworks show from the nearby Blue Wahoos Stadium. As the popularity increased, so does the challenge to find parking so Kathleen and I decided to pull into a local lot and fork out the $5 entrance fee. As we waited for a spot, a grumpy old man in a car full of similarly grumpy people approached us. Taking instructions from the lot attendant, all of us had our windows down and as we approached the car, I heard him making some disparaging comments about my wife's driving. Well, nobody messes with my wife so I reached deep into my cranium for a quick-witted comeback to put this offender in his place and both my wife and I were shocked at what came out. "You're stupid!" I shouted as we pulled abeam his car and continued to our space. Kathleen and I laughed for the rest of the night at my less-than-well-spun comeback and reversion to my inner 10-year-old.

As of today, Collin is a fortnight into his driving years and although the car bug has bitten big, he is still without. But it's not for lack of trying on his part. He and his brother Alex found a "sweet ride" up just over the Alabama border and we went to check it out last weekend. Because I am not known for my haggling skills, it was decided that Collin would be the lead negotiator and I'd be there just for moral support. Well after a long drive up to the sticks, our destination was marked by the car we came to see parked out front. As the owner came out to greet us, the first thing that came out of my young wheeler and dealer's mouth was, "I love it!" So much for a poker face and so began an interesting three days of car ownership which ended after the title turned out to be in less than good order.

July 2013

In my flying days, before we hit the runway, we would check the weather and then, if flying outside of the local area, the NOTAMS. This stood for Notice to Airmen which would warn of any potential hazards along a flight path or at a location that could affect the safety of the flight. With that in mind, after the second try, Collin is mobile. After our mechanic checked out the last potential car and gave it two thumbs down, he showed us a car he took as a trade for future services. Next thing you know, Collin is the proud owner of a 2003 Saturn station wagon or as he calls it, his "Swag Wagon." I've got to say it is very sharp…not the station wagon of yore but sleek and low and just big enough for his surfboard to ride inside. There is no driving equivalent of a NOTAM but if you see a shiny white Saturn with a skinny teenager sporting a huge grin at the wheel, please give it a wide berth.

Along with the car came a trip to Regions bank where we opened our son's first bank account. Since the lad is now a pseudo-adult, he got a lesson in money management. From now on, his paycheck doesn't get stashed in the wallet where it finds frivolous places to go without a second thought. It goes into the bank where it's linked to dad's account and the first $30 per month goes to cover ½ of the car insurance and the remainder grows into an emergency account to cover the inevitable expenses that come from the joy of owning stuff. I will say that Kathleen and I do enjoy our boy's new independence. That first night when he was able to head off to work on his own was a pretty neat milestone and another baby step for us on our road to being empty nesters...I think I just leaked a happiness tear.

The summer is going well for Alex. He is stepping up his hours at work (Taco Bell) and he has a new obsession with weight lifting. As far as we know, this isn't female induced but then again, Alex doesn't tell us that sort of thing... might have something to do with this newsletter. Anyhow, our boy is cranking it out on the weights every other day and the funny thing is how different things have become over the years. When I was his age, I joined Pep's Gym, an infamously grungy gym downtown and got my tips from the power-lifters and other gym-rats. Alex, in contrast, gets all his workouts from google-ing. Well, I guess all that matters is results and the kid is getting dangerously close to a 3-pack.

A couple weeks back, I took Collin to my Rotary meeting under the guise of buying him lunch. Unbeknownst to the boy, I wanted him to be our weekly speaker and tell us about his recent experience at the Rotary Youth Leadership camp. He met me at my office and we left in his new car. After greasing him up with a trip to the gas station, I told him about his speaking engagement. He surprised me and didn't complain. At lunch, when the time came, I gave him the option of just staying at his seat but he surprised me again and took the podium. He did great, poised and relaxed, even more impressive since he had no prep whatsoever. This kid just might make it out there…I'll keep you posted.

As for myself, I recently had some doubts. A newly retired, longtime and dear client came to see me about rolling over her old 403(b). Shortly after sitting down, she said she wanted to show me something. She reached into her purse and pulled out her new handgun and let me know that it was loaded. Believe it or not, this hasn't happened to me before so I kiddingly asked if she was going to shoot me (the market had had an off week). I had written about going to the shooting range so she just wanted to show me her new toy. The best part of this career is that every day is unique!

August 2013

Sitting on the 23rd chromosome, nestled between the no guts no glory and the holy #!@it gene, is the adventure gene. Mine has been hyperactive since birth. I blame it for causing me to join the Navy after Business School instead of getting a real job. I've always been jealous when I read stories of the boy flying a Cessna across the country, the girl sailing solo across the Atlantic, or the young man attempting to climb all the world's highest mountain peaks. I love the whole "man-versus-nature", "because it's there" thing. To that end, when I booked a spot at this year's YMCA General Assembly in Philadelphia, I immediately put thought into how I could convince Kathleen to let me attend via motorcycle. Under the heading of it's easier to ask forgiveness than permission, I spent a few minutes on the "just do it" option but decided that returning home a week later to an empty house wasn't a risk I was willing to take, adventure gene or not. So, on a quiet Sunday morning, I made my pitch and after about an hour and revisiting our Estate Planning binder, I got the reluctant thumbs up.

The journey went well and at the conference, besides meeting YMCA leadership from around the country and getting updated on the state of the movement, we were treated to some first-rate speakers. Dr. Sanjay Gupta of CNN fame gave a fascinating presentation on health and nutrition. He spoke of the residents of Okinawa (home to the world's largest concentration of centenarians) and two take-away concepts that help explain why. "Eat until you are 80% full" (or hara hachi-bu) is the advice that Okinawan grandmothers have given for years as well as finding your Iki Gai, or "a reason for being" which they believe brings true joy, inner satisfaction and a meaning to life. After the 3-day conference and a reunion with former Navy friend Michael, his wife Shannon and their two beautiful daughters. Post Navy, Michael found his way to Chick-fil-A and is a highly successful restaurant operator. He's also a fellow motorcycle rider so we took an obligatory after-dinner ride along the gorgeous northern Maryland country side. Finally, I reunited with my riding partner Tom for an uneventful and soggy trip home.

September 2013

Of course, Elvis never needed protection, who didn't love the guy. I chose this quote on August 16th, my wife's 50th birthday and the 33rd anniversary of the death of the King. You'd better believe Elvis had some good CPA's; in 1956, his breakout year, the marginal tax rate for an individual making a million dollars was 89%! Unfortunately, he never hitched up with a Certified Financial Planner. If he had, he would have been steered to an Estate Planning Attorney which would have made things a lot easier for his family. When he left us in 1977, his estate was valued at more than $10 million. A poorly constructed will led to a toxic probate process that dragged on for more than 12 years. In the end, taxes and legal fees took more than 70%, leaving just $2.7 million to Presley's family. Other than some very bad plastic surgery and a marriage to Michael Jackson, the family turned out ok but it's my job to keep your families from surprises like that.

Kathleen just completed her 50th trip around the sun and to celebrate, we tacked 2 ½ days onto the back end of a business trip to San Francisco and got a taste of how they do things on the Left Coast. Wow! I grew up in Massachusetts, the East Coast version of California and it took me about 30 years to make a political transition to the center/right so this trip to the extreme left was eye opening. On our first day, we decided to walk on the wild side and took the bus to Haight Ashbury for breakfast. Afterwards, we walked off our meal by strolling through Golden Gate Park. It was a beautiful Saturday morning, and we tried not to inhale as we passed the hippies camped out at the park's entrance...I think I saw my youngest brother Josh. We then stumbled upon Peace in the Park, a Festival of Spirit just past Nancy Pelosi Drive. Talk about people watching! We closed out the afternoon with a boat ride to Alcatraz Island for a tour of the eponymous penitentiary. One time home to Al Capone, Machine Gun Kelly and Robert Straud, better known as the Birdman, the tour was fascinating, a bit creepy and the boat ride made for some of the best views of the city and the famous bridge, which Kathleen's grandfather actually helped build.

We worked off Sunday's breakfast on a bicycle ride across the Golden Gate Bridge to the beautiful town of Sausalito. After a quick bite, we caught a bus across the famous Hwy 1 (I wish I was on the motorcycle!) up to Muir Woods National Park, home to some of the world's tallest and oldest trees, the giant Redwoods or Sequoias. Some of these bad boys stand over 250 feet and are over 1200 years old. We worked that night's dinner off by walking back to our hotel up and down San Francisco's famous hills. The night ended with a "Kagan" moment when we walked a few blocks past our destination and ended up in a rather seedy part of town. Kathleen had been questioning me which made me even more intent that we were on the right path, right up until the nice man offered to sell us some crystal meth. We turned around and picked up the pace when his nice friend, sensing maybe that meth wasn't our "poison" of choice, made a similar offer for some really good "acid". Our trip was complete! Special thanks to Uncle Boo for the excellent restaurant choices and John Smithies for the outstanding Belgian Beer joint.

This school year is a bit different for Alex, now a High School Senior. In addition to his Advanced Placement courses, he's taking a class at the local State College through the dual enrollment program and he's really digging it. The boy is looking and acting so grown up I can't get that Harry Chapin song out of my head. It's just about time to get those college applications out. Alex has known for years that he wants to get into some sort of engineering and the University of Florida is still his first choice but we did hear that state schools in Alabama, in an effort to bump up their engineering programs, are offering students with a 30 on their ACT test, a tuition-free engineering education. Can you say "Roll Tide!"

October 2013

"I believe in the dignity of labor, whether with head or hand; that the world owes no man a living but it owes every man an opportunity to make a living."

John D. Rockefeller

When I brag on our kids at the office, I pull out a spinning picture cube with photos of both boys and ask my clients if they can tell who is the future engineer and who is the surfer. So far, they're batting 100%! Collin, the surfer, is by no means an academic slouch and when he focuses, he puts out some amazing work. He is extremely "Right brained", which is the creative hemisphere, and his skills really shine when he puts pen to paper. When I proofread his recent essay on surfing the perfect wave, I was shocked and actually thought the lad may have plagiarized from the Surfing mag that was lying on the desk beside the computer. He assured me it wasn't the case and he did snag on A on the effort.

It's a bit sad that we get suspicious of superior achievement. Our nephew Benjamin, a High School Senior up in Burlington Vermont, recently got mail from the folks who administer the SAT. It turned out he did so well on the test that they thought there must've been some sort of mischief at play. They gave him several options to respond, including retaking the test in a controlled environment. He chose to write back and his extremely eloquent reply put their suspicions to bed. Benjamin is not sure where he'll be studying, but he is sure that a career in Medicine is in his future. Selfishly, I hope it's in geriatrics.

November 2013

Collin experienced his own partial shutdown this month. It was homecoming and he took his date out for the obligatory pre-dance dinner. He went big and got some fondue at the Melting Pot which left him quite a bit lighter in the wallet. No worries except that it left no moolah for gas for the upcoming week so his car sat in the driveway for most of the following school week. Great lesson in deficit spending although Collin did get a partial bailout from our soon-to-be-former neighbor with a big heart and full gas can.

Friday the 13th has always been a lucky day for us since first born Alex's birth 18 Octobers ago. Kathleen and I still can't wrap our arms around the fact that our boy is technically a man and could run away to the Marine Corps any time he chooses. It's not an issue at this time since he just got word of his scholarship to University of Alabama but he and his bud (also a newly minted "man") commemorated with a special ceremony on our back porch. I snapped a picture of them smoking cigars (it won't be a habit and there was no bourbon) to ring in the occasion.

December 2013

"I can calculate the movement of the stars, but not the madness of men."

Sir Isaac Newton

Kathleen, Alex, and I made another trip to Tuscaloosa last month. We caught our first Alabama football game thanks to our friends Jim and Anne who so graciously offered their tickets and hotel room. Now that was an experience. The cool temps and drizzly weather did nothing at all to dampen our enthusiasm, nor that of the capacity crowd at this, the last home game of the year, which also made it the last home game ever played by this year's seniors. They didn't disappoint. After 60 minutes of play, the Tide did some major rolling, taking down the University of Tennessee at Chattanooga 49 to nothing! Alex still hasn't officially committed but he did buy a hat and my motorcycle is proudly sporting a new sticker on the saddlebag.

Collin got the results of his first college prep test, the ACT, knocking out a 28 which is exactly what big brother Alex got on his first try. I've always told Collin that he's smarter than his big brother, he just doesn't try as hard or care as much. I'm happy to say it's got him a bit pumped to look more seriously into the College thing as a parallel option to the Coast Guard. Not surprisingly, the test also showed him to be well suited to a career that takes advantage of his outgoing nature like business or the travel and hospitality industry. Add in the surfing component and I can see visiting our son at his gig at the Four Seasons Maui or the Hilton in Tahiti. I'll keep you posted.

The traditional gift for a 20th anniversary is China so it was perfectly fitting that Kathleen and I spent our anniversary eve at our favorite Chinese restaurant with the couple that made us possible. Bob and Tessa Burns introduced us almost 21 years ago when Bob and I reconnected as helicopter flight instructors at Whiting Field. Our first group date was a bowling outing and the rest, as they say, is history. More than twenty years later, we all look exactly the same (of course) and the Burns' oldest is a Sophomore at the US Naval Academy. Bob still flies helicopters for a living and is getting ready to move the remaining clan to College Station, TX for his new gig as an EMS pilot. We will miss them but look forward to a road trip in the near future. As for an actual anniversary gift, I chose rubber and put 4 new tires on my bride's car...safety first.

Fish tales

High school grad

Montreal 2004

The boys in the woods

Collin's Prom

2014

February 2014

"There is no medicine like hope, no incentive so great, and no tonic so powerful as expectation of something better tomorrow."

Orison Swett Marden

A fellow New Englander, Orison's childhood was marked by tragedy and gave him little reason to be hopeful. When he was just three years old, his mother died and four years later, his father's death left him and his two sisters orphans. They would spend their childhood being shuttled from one guardian to another with young Orison working as a "hired boy" to earn their keep. But a serendipitous discovery in an old attic turned his life around. The book, titled, "Self-Help" by Scottish author Samuel Smiles (how appropriate) gave the young teenager the inspiration and motivation to take charge of his destiny and set his sights on a future limited only by his imagination. He would go on to achieve degrees from the likes of Andover, Boston University and Harvard. This self-made man and self-help author would lay the foundation that would later be built upon by Dale Carnegie, Norman Vincent Peale, Stephen Covey and Tony Robbins.

It was an inevitable event for someone that I've got to admit, has turned into quite a handsome young man. Collin has a girlfriend. How the creative young lad accomplished the "ask" is even cooler than the fact that she is a senior and a Captain on the cheerleading team. Collin is a decent basketball player and his then potential girlfriend, had been a starter on the girls Varsity team. So, the boy's plan was to ask her to play some one-on-one at the local Community Center. When they pulled up to the facility, Collin offered his rival a headband with the proposal inscribed in black sharpie. To those dads out there with daughters, I know that my pride reflects a humongous double standard and if it was my daughter on the other end of this story, I might have written it differently. But I am proud to say that Kathleen and I have raised a gentleman.

For the husband's out there, please tell me this has happened to you too. Kathleen had been bugging me to tackle a small home improvement project for about 6 months. The drywall above the shower enclosure in the boys' bathroom had some water damage which I'd repaired in a less than optimal manner about a year back. Kathleen wanted me to put up some tile there to fix the issue permanently. I like a good project at least as much as the next guy, so I wasn't entirely averse to the prospect of a weekend in the loo. Here's the rub. Apparently, in a dream she had, during a home-improvement project done by yours truly, I did a particularly shoddy job and when questioned by her, I was less than courteous. That settled it, we had to have a professional tackle this job. It's a good thing we're so in love or I don't know how I'd feel about the fact that my wife lets the "dream" me rule her decision making.

March 2014

I know this will disappoint some folks out there...even a neighbor or two. Alex was accepted to Florida. Now this wasn't a surprise to me...I would've put money on it. The surprise is that his best bud was accepted as well. Now he has to make the choice between Alabama and Florida. The good news is that there's really not a wrong answer. He'll get a fantastic education at either school. He will come out with an engineering degree and likely have a great career waiting at the end of his four years of study. The problem is what to do with all the Alabama paraphernalia we've collected over the past five months if he chooses Florida. I'll keep you all in the loop.

I will admit that I'm a sensitive man but I try to at least put out an attempt at manliness here and there. There's the moustache, the motorcycle, the license to carry. During a recent manly pursuit, my Saturday morning motorcycle ride with the regular gang…a group of guys in their late 50's to mid-60's, I noticed Bill had the tell-tale signs of a round of Effudex. I know because it's an unpleasant routine that I go through every couple of years to battle the self-inflicted, sun-damaged stupidity on my scary mug. For those lucky enough to not have heard of this- stuff, Effudex is a topical chemotherapy used to treat pre-cancer and basal cell "crusties" that pop up on us middle-ager's faces, arms, back, etc. It's about a month of pain and ugliness. Another of our group recommended that as an alternative, I go see their "person" instead. She and her husband have been getting this treatment for years and have avoided the month of pain. I decided to give it a try; if it was good enough for Hank (a real "manly" man), it's good enough for me. I scheduled the appointment and, on my way, I called my brother for support. "You're getting a facial you woman!" was his reply. I guess he was right but I did ride my motorcycle in a manly way to the appointment.

April 2014

L ast month I joined Club Five-Oh. A friend wished me a good day and I told her it's been great so far. I woke up and had a good bowel movement, the two most important things for us club members at this point in the game. My wife gave me Jimmy Buffett's best seller, "A Pirate Looks at Fifty." Great read so far. The colorful Mr. Buffett, who flunked out of college on his first go-around, is now valued at over $400 million. Not quite Warren Buffett but not bad for a kid from Pascagoula. Talk about finding your unique brand. That in a nutshell, is the secret of life. Find out where you fit in the grand scheme. How you can do something that fills a need, that benefits others, and that can support a lifestyle that will satisfy your needs. That's something both Mr. Buffett's (Jimmy & Warren) have figured out and we can all learn from them.

I'd never tell him, but when I think of our first-born son Alex, I don't think athlete. He is a thinker. His buddies used to call him the "brain" and I often turn to him for his opinion because I know it will be all logic and nearly devoid of emotion. But wouldn't you know, in the twilight of his youth, he's thrown us a curveball. Our boy is quite an accomplished pole vaulter on the High School track team. He's number one on the team and third in the district and it's an absolute gas to watch. I'm still chalking it up to his brain. Pole vaulting is nothing more than a skinny kid with a long stick doing geometry on the run and in that sense, Al is in his element.

Now for the flip side. I'd never tell him but when I think of Collin, I don't think student. Don't get me wrong, the kid is incredibly gifted but there are lots of things he'd rather do than study, get a colonoscopy for instance. But just when you think you've got 'm all figured out, the boy brought home a second consecutive all "A" report card. Best I can tell, he's seeing his big brother face the end of one chapter (high school) and the beginning of a bigger one, and he's seeing his not-so-distant future. Where'd that "brain" come from?

As for the future, Al has yet to share with us his choice of college. Recall that he's been accepted to the engineering schools of Florida and Alabama. He has until May 1st to make the decision and I've left him alone because every time mom asks, he politely tells her to buzz off. It's his journey. Collin has submitted his application to the US Coast Guard Academy AIM summer program. If selected he will experience the "rigor, discipline, and rewards of the Academy, just like a cadet, for a week in July." In recent years, one third of the next year's incoming class attended this program so Collin is anxiously awaiting their decision which should come sometime in May. I'll keep you posted.

May 2014

ᶜᵃᵖᵗᶦᵒⁿ

"*One recognizes one's course by discovering the paths that stray from it.*"

Albert Camus

Roll Tide! I was beginning to think I'd have to water-board him to make his college decision, but a dinner outing did the trick. Alex spilled the beans as we watched the sunset over Pensacola Bay, relaxing at Jaco's on Palafox Pier. Alex is Bama bound. He is very excited and so are we. He will pursue a degree in engineering and a career he was built for. Watching Alex crank out his calculus homework last night, I looked over his shoulder and said, "ouch", flashing back to my semester of business calc at UMass in the days of the abacas. He just dryly replied, "it's easy", which brought a little lump in my throat as I realized that when he hits the road for Tuscaloosa this September, if everything works out, he's only coming back for holidays.

If you haven't been to the Aloha Grill in Gulf Breeze, you are missing out. Excellent menu, great service, reasonable prices. And now, behind the scenes, the Kagan brothers are doing their part to enhance your dining experience. Collin is into his second year on the payroll and has moved up from chief-dishwasher to cook. He's loving his upgraded role and has even used his latest skills at home, working up an outstanding blackened grouper the other night. Alex is the newest team member, leaving his long-held spot in corporate America (Taco Bell) for a second-act with a family "start-up." He loves the new gig and I'm sure he's using his analytical skills to bring new efficiencies to the dish-washing crew. Stop in and tell them I sent you.

If the Coast Guard doesn't work out, Collin is going to be in sales of some sort. He's never met a stranger and is constantly pitching a deal. But we recently had a good conversation on business terminology that I hope he takes with him in the future. He pitched me a deal where I lend him money for a car repair and he pays me back weekly until the debt is retired. "What's in it for me?", I asked, sharing that an offer has something for both parties. He was looking for a favor not a deal. "A deal would be, I loan you the money, you pay me back, and instead of interest, you'd wash the cars every week until the debt is retired." In the end, I granted him the favor…I'm getting soft in my 5th decade.

You don't know what you've got till it's gone. I'm with you Joni Mitchell. But it's not a Big Yellow Taxi that took away my old lady, it's Annie's 80th birthday. They are on day 5 of a 12-day, bucket-list trip to Arizona with her 4 grown kids and younger brother. Annie is definitive proof that 80 is the new 45. This adventure includes rafting down the Colorado River, hiking to several canyons, and bungee jumping off Glen Canyon Dam Bridge (ok, I made the last one up but you get the picture!) We're keeping up with the adventure on Facebook and random texts and it looks like they are having a National Lampoon movie-worthy time.

Me and the boys, on the other hand, are struggling through and missing our old-lady tremendously. Thanks to new neighbors Robert and Theresa for dinner last night, we just ran out of Vienna Sausages.

It's always nice to reconnect with old friends and reminisce about the glory days. Last month, old Navy buddy Gary, wife Mo, and daughters Kate and Jessica came south from Atlanta for Spring Break. We had a great time catching up on all that's happened since their last visit and reliving some old Navy adventures (there's a future book in there somewhere). Outside of his career in manufacturing, Gary is an accomplished musician. He's a singer/songwriter/guitar player. He shipped us an advance copy of the new CD, signed of course, that he'd been working on for about 20 years and we jammed to the classics of Gary Stelzel and Collision Course. But the best part of the visit came while we watched the NCAA Basketball Semi-Final game. Gary's beloved Wisconsin Badgers, in their first semifinal appearance in about 50 years, faced the Kentucky Wildcats. Gary paced the room nervously like an expectant father awaiting word on his first-born child (ok, in the old days when dads waited outside). The great part is that, in my sons' eyes, I'm now the second most obnoxious person to watch sports with. Thanks Gary!

June 2014

> *"Everyone has a game plan, until they get punched in the face."*
>
> Mike Tyson

For me, it hasn't entirely sunken in. Kathleen said that she was feeling numb all weekend. Our eldest son Alex is a High School graduate. He heads to the University of Alabama in less than three months to begin a study of engineering. I haven't changed the locks yet, one more in High School, but next time this year I'll be looking at plans to convert their bedrooms into something. Maybe a woodworking shop.

Poor Collin. His 17th birthday fell smack dab in the middle of Alex's big week. Talk about no respect. Adding insult to injury, rather than a birthday hug from his favorite dad, as he emerged from his boy-cave, he walked directly into a tirade from yours truly for some minor infraction that I really can't remember anymore. Just another example of "Life Ain't Fair." To be fair, when I remembered that it was his birthday, around lunchtime, I called him right away and gave a double-dose of phone hugs. I am very proud of our youngest son. With school out, he's really stepped up his work schedule. This morning he showed us his biggest paycheck ever, $193 for one hellacious week of work. I was quick to show him that 52 weeks of that schedule would produce a massive $10,036 annual income. Stay in school my son.

Finally, a sad note. Going back to the Tyson quote, I took one to the jaw early last month when Evelyn, my office manager since "forever" said she'd like to retire. Finally empty-nesters, she and husband John decided it's time to focus on their together time. I forced myself to expedite the grieving process and once settled on acceptance, I began the process of replacing an irreplaceable partner who's been with me through thick and thin. I told Evelyn that the worst part for her is leaving with our practice in full stride...kind of like the first wife who stayed with her husband through medical school. Now she's leaving just as I complete my surgical residency and have to bring in the trophy wife. Well, I'm happy to say that things are working out well. Our new Office Manager will be someone that I've known, respected and worked with for about six years. Sandy Crow has 14 years of experience in bookkeeping and accounting and most recently worked for a local firm. We are excited to have her onboard and Evelyn is busy bringing her up to speed on our policies and procedures. Evelyn will stick around in a different capacity, filling in for Sandy and working with us on special projects as needed. I will miss having her around on a daily basis but am very excited for her and John to start their next chapter.

July 2014

"Here is the test to find whether your mission on earth is finished: If you're alive, it isn't."

Richard Bach

Richard Bach wrote Jonathan Livingston Seagull in 1970. I will never forget seeing the movie with my dad in 1973. I was nine years old, the first of three boys, and I lived to make my father proud. The film was about a rogue gull, bored with everyday seagull life, and looking to find something to feed his adrenaline habit. Pushing flight to the limit, he became the bird version of Chuck Yeager. He would be banished for his derring-do but later find contentment in mentoring other such outcasts. We shared a name, which today, I only here when talking with my folks. Like the bird's pop, my old man would often shake his head and say, "Jonathan, Jonathan, Jonathan," to suggest that I may be heading in a less-than-productive direction. I love you pop.

I came home for a late lunch about the same time Collin was pulling into the driveway. The wind had really been kicking so I knew the surf was up and asked him how it went. With a forlorn look of someone who's life was temporarily out of his control, he said he had no idea. He hadn't been to the beach. He'd just returned from a movie…and a chick flick at that. Girlfriend management is tough stuff.

We brought Alex up to Tuscaloosa for his freshman orientation at the University of Alabama. We didn't get to leave him yet but he did sign up for all of his classes. The little stinker even went and declared his major. It looks like we've been growing a future civil engineer for 18 years. He's very excited about everything which of course makes us all the more excited for him. Someone not so excited is younger brother Collin. With Alex pushing off in just over a month, Collin seems to be going out of his way to hang out with big-brother this summer. Though he's camouflaged it pretty well in his teenage years, Collin has always loved his bro and when they were toddlers, he'd do anything to make Alex happy. I think it's going to be pretty tough on the lad, which is kind of touching to a mom and dad. Of course, it might just be the fact that he's realized that he's going to have to deal with 100% of our attention for the next year and that is absolutely terrifying!

The boys and I have done some special bonding over the past 5 weeks. I sold all of the big-boy toys we'd acquired over the years that hadn't been getting used. The proceeds funded the purchase of a couple of used trail-bikes. We've gone riding in the woods in the north part of our county every Sunday since and have had an absolute blast. There's nothing that bonds a dad and his boys better than sharing the man-versus-nature-versus-machine conflict. We had a fantastic Father's Day ride and I even called my dad on the way up to make it multi-generational.

Life is hard, it's certainly not fair, and you've heard the tired cliché that it didn't come with instructions. I'd like to challenge that contention. If human nature is fairly consistent throughout the ages, what better instruction manual could you ask for, than reading the biographies of those who've done it right. Choose your hero. I'm a big fan of Moses, Jesus, Lincoln, and Bob Bell. Bob has threatened us with an autobiography for years and he's finally delivered. "Un Moving Four Ward, Tales & Tips for Keeping Perspective Despite Life's Challenges" is his story and after reading it, you will feel guilty for ever asking, "why me?" Since Bob's college accident left him in a wheelchair 25 years ago, he's been a CPA for a major firm, earned his law degree and worked as a hotshot securities attorney on Wall Street, and become a College Professor. In between his professional achievements, he's travelled the world and spent time in 38 countries, although he admits on the book's back cover that "he's never worked as a DJ at a strip club". His book is a must read for anyone who's ever faced, is currently facing, or will be facing adversity…in other words, it's for everyone. You can order your copy from bobbellbooks.com and it will come signed.

August 2014

"I don't think of work as work and play as play. It's all living."

Richard Branson

It's a beautiful thing to witness your kids transform into real people. I'm not talking about the body hair and growth spurts. Pets do that. I mean the rational thinking and emotional maturity stuff. Collin had his first real girlfriend this year. She was a sweetheart. Smart, attractive, and an upper-classman who graduated High School in May. Frankly, her only flaw was settling for my son as her beau (just kidding). But that son is a realist and made the tough call that it didn't make sense to keep the relationship going while she went off to college and he was busy planning for his next act. So, he initiated the breakup, his first. It was tough, he got emotional, and felt bad because she felt bad. You might think it's a bit odd, but I was happy that he was sad. Empathy is an under-appreciated trait and I rank it right up there with intelligence, passion, and ambition. I love it that our son has it in abundance. It's going to serve him well down the road.

September 2014

> *"Life isn't fair, unless you were born in America."*
>
> Collin's Psychology Teacher

My kids have been blessed with some exceptional educators, and 15 years of client interviews back up this month's quote-smith. The undeniable truth about our great nation is, despite ranting from some in the media, everyone has the opportunity to be and do whatever their imagination suggests. I am not denying that some have a bigger challenge than others due to circumstances beyond their control, but in my humble opinion, current laws and policies make up for those inequities. So to those who lament over their current station in life, I recommend turning off the TV and stop looking for reasons why you can't succeed. It's up to you, formulate a plan and execute. If you need help, find a mentor. Most folks who've found success are more than happy to share their stories and more often than not, they are repeatable.

Roll Tide! Alex is at Alabama. We made the trip in two cars. Al & brother Collin in one, me and Kathleen in the other. I'd imagine the conversations were very different. The boys talking parties, girls, football, and no doubt some "remember when's?" While Kathleen and I were actually pretty quiet, each in our own little world, reliving memories of our first-born's first 18. I couldn't help but throw out an occasional story (fable?!) from my glory days at the University of Massachusetts. And then an old song came on the radio that brought tears to us both. Memories of then two and half year-old Alex singing said song while doing his signature dance moves were just too much.

Just to make sure we pegged out the emotion-meter, the move-in fell on Kathleen's birthday. With the move in complete, the boys gave mom her present, a pair of charms for her bracelet. It was time for a quick walk around campus so Alex could show his little brother the quad, football stadium and of course, the library. Then we hit the strip to grab some lunch. Kathleen and I had a beer to prepare for what came after lunch. We walked back from town, across the grassy quad, to the parking lot where we said our goodbyes. There wasn't a dry eye in the bunch. The four most wet belonged to mom and little brother, although if you ask Collin, it was allergies. I've got about 3,500 hours of pilot-in-command time in helicopters, but I've vowed to do my damndest not to be a helicopter dad. I made it about 15 minutes before sending my first text (had to tell my boy how very proud I was), and called him that night (had to troubleshoot his laptop). We head to Tuscaloosa this Friday for parents' weekend, which includes a football game. More to follow.

October 2014

Those who've followed Soundings know that I have a passion for anything and everything motorcycle. I've ridden for over 35 years and though I tried to quit after marrying a motorcycle-phobe, I quickly realized it was part of my DNA. I recently returned from a trip of a lifetime... bucket list stuff. I joined a group of about 20 that flew to Munich to spend 8 days touring the Alps on rented BMW's. It was absolutely fantastic! As we navigated the un-paralleled twisties, and basked in the glory of spectacular mountain vistas and rolling green meadows, I tapped into my inner Zen. I pondered how many of the qualities that made our trip a success were the same that lead to financial happiness. I thought it would be fun to combine this month's Market Commentary with my Personal Page. I'm writing this missive at 36,000 feet above the Atlantic Ocean, on a westerly course south of Reykjavik, Iceland, fighting the Jetstream and making a sluggish 471 mph groundspeed. Humor me as I make my case.

Nearly Anything is possible with a little planning. I would have never dreamed that I'd be in the Holy Land of motorcycling, with a half dozen legendary mountain passes (including the epic Stelvio) indelibly stamped on my rider's resume. About a year ago, I returned from the bike shop with a flyer that I shared with Kathleen. I was shocked when she said, "why don't you go?" She suggested I put away money on a monthly basis and make it happen. Who would have thought? What initially seemed like an impossible dream, was actually quite attainable with a little time, discipline, and planning. Sound like retirement to anyone?

Don't underestimate the value of Guidance. During our 8-day adventure, we travelled more than 1,500 miles through four countries, and three languages. Other than an occasional spin on the Autobahn, we stuck to the back country. I could not get Julie Andrews and those doggone Von Trapp kids' music out of my head. Other than my wife, the only thing I enjoy more than riding is travelling but I could not have done this without our guide. Martin had over 40 years of riding experience in these parts. He was unflappable and took us to places that we'd never have found on a map. At the same time, when things got hairy, we trusted his skill and experience to get us safely to our night's destination. When it comes to navigating your financial journey, a trusted guide can give you the same comfort and confidence needed to make it to your destination even when the roads get "twisty", allowing you to focus on what's important and enjoy the scenery along the way.

Look ahead and make light inputs. Google Stelvio Pass and watch a video or two from the list that populates. It was a truly magnificent experience that engages all of your senses

- even taste, if you stop for a pre-ascent cappuccino down bottom, and a tasty bratwurst at the peak. When riding in the mountains, it's critically important to look ahead and anticipate terrain changes and potential obstacles. What's behind you really doesn't matter. The crazy Italian riders that rocket past you on their Ducati's and Moto Guzzi's are not going to get you hurt. Not anticipating that left-hand hairpin turn or Audi sports car that jumped on his brakes will. The bikes we rode are truly marvels of engineering. They don't ride themselves, but over the years, they've been designed and tweaked to do everything possible to make our job easier. I found myself getting into trouble only when I got tense or made unnecessary control inputs rather than settle in and let the bike do most of the work. The same case can be made for investing. We can learn from the rear-view mirror but decisions need to be made based on what's up the road. When adjustments need to be made, it usually pays to keep your inputs light, and purposeful. Over-controlling is often just as dangerous to your financial goals as it is your riding.

Sometimes you've got to be aggressive to be safe. Traffic roundabout are pretty uncommon in the States but they are a way of life in Europe. At a four-way intersection, rather than waiting on a traffic light, you enter the roundabout and exit in the desired direction. I love them, but you can't be hesitant or you will get yourself and others in trouble. You've probably heard that there are roads in Germany that do not have a speed limit. At one point on the autobahn, we clocked 205 kilometers per hour (about 127 mph). Surprisingly, in all of our travels, I only saw one accident. The Europeans understand driving and the fact that sometimes, the best defense is a good offense.

I often hear folks say that they don't want to take any risk. They are talking about market risk and it's understandable given what we've all been through over the past 15 years. The problem is risk takes many shapes. One of the biggest is longevity risk or the possibility of having more years of life than dollars in your bank account. It's wonderful that medicine is advancing to the point that 80 is truly becoming the new 60. My favorite mother-in-law will be 81 in March and is still working nearly full-time. Not because she has to, but because she wants to. If she was in a Union shop, they'd probably threaten her for making the rest of them look like slackers! If you can accomplish your lifestyle goals without taking market risk, great. Unfortunately, most of us need more growth or income than is currently available in "safe" investments. And when you take longevity, interest-rate, and inflation risk into account, the traditionally "riskier" assets start looking more suitable.

Prepare for the Weather. In late September, early October, the weather was always going to be our wildcard. For the adventure rider (Netflix subscribers should check out "Long Way Round" and "Long Way Down" for a couple of fun miniseries), that's actually part of the appeal. Anyone can ride when it's nice, but what separates the men from the boys is staying out there when it gets crappy. Of course, being prepared is everything. Knowing that we could see everything from blue skies and 70 degrees, to 30's and sleet in the mountains, we all made darn sure we were prepared. Rain gear, long johns, two pairs of gloves, and a good set of boots and I was ready for anything and everything. It turned out that the maker of the weather was good to us… thanks God! It was fabulous for Stelvio and I took some fantastic pictures and video. We had one day of riding in the rain and it was actually fun to test our foul weather riding skills.

When it comes to investing, no-one needs reminding that there will be storms. But just as the threat of weather didn't deter us from our journey, it shouldn't prevent you from financial success. The best way to prepare is to have a plan. Your plan should be designed to get you from where you are, to where you need to be, with the understanding that there will be bumps in the road and storms on the horizon. Our financial planning software has gotten so good that we can look at how well your plan will weather anything from an afternoon shower to a full-blown hurricane. If we haven't done a stress-test or you know someone that's unsure of the roadworthiness of their plan, give us a call and we will give it an evaluation.

Always remember what is important. Sadly, we had a mishap on day 3. A member of our group was an inexperienced rider. She had come along with her husband and rather than riding as a passenger, she insisted on getting her own motorcycle. She had trouble from the start and our guides and her husband tried to get her to enjoy the trip as a passenger. She was steadfast and determined, and let her ego get in the way of both common sense and the big picture. While riding up a mountain pass, she struck the side of the mountain and went over the handlebars of her bike. She was going relatively slowly but even so, the bike landed on her leg, breaking it in two places. She needed to be medevac'd off the mountain by a helicopter and had surgery a couple days later. She is doing fine and will likely make a full recovery but the lesson learned can be applied to investing as well. She lost sight of the big picture and what brings true enjoyment to life.

Regarding finances, I often see people getting hung up on the dollars as if it's a contest to see how much can be accumulated rather than looking at what is truly important to them. Will you have the lifestyle that you want? Can you do the things that you want to do with and for the people that you care about? It should be about the tangible as well as intangible things that make life worth living. If we haven't had a discovery or rediscovery meeting, give me a call and we'll set one up either in person or on the phone. I think you'll find it a worthwhile exercise.

November 2014

"Unbroken happiness is a bore; it should have ups and downs."

Moliere

Collin pushed submit on his online application to the US Coast Guard Academy. It's all over but the waiting. Early admission is between now and December 24th, so he's hoping for a really nice Christmas present from Uncle Sam. I think he's got a good chance. It's very, very competitive but the young lad has the grades, he's not un-charming or bad on the eyes either. I was out of town but he made me proud by attending, on his own, an open-house at the Coast Guard Air Station in Mobile. Our squared-away young man arrived more than an hour early and got some semi-private, quality time with the Admission Officer who flew down for the event. Needless to say, he's excited but has a plan B, C, and D in place just in case it's not in the cards. I've got to say that Collin is really coming into his own now that he's out of the shadow of his big brother.

Speaking of our eldest, Alex turned nineteen since the last edition. I can't believe he's almost a non-teenager. First semester at the University of Alabama is going well and he's got himself a nice routine. His grades are solid, all A's and B's so far after an initial scare on his first Calculus exam. We are very impressed with the University. Alex's Engineering professors have engaged him completely and he's already thinking past his four years of "time-out" to what he'll be doing in the real world. As I type, big Al is home for an extra-long weekend, and he didn't even bring home his laundry! On his first night home, Kathleen asked what he'd like for dinner. I was prepping for my colonoscopy and Collin was working, so it was just going to be the two of them. She gave him the choice of going out to a restaurant, bringing home some takeout, or anything else his heart desired. Well, the kid definitely got smarter in his short time at the University. "Could you make your tacos," was his request. Given the rare choice of anything conceivable, he chose mom's home-cooking. That's called "street smarts."

December 2014

We humans have a bit of a narcissist streak. Our favorite subject is often the reflection in the mirror. I recently got a lesson in humility. After the funeral of the mother of an old friend, the attendees gathered outside the church on a cool Saturday morning. It was a large crowd, the deceased a long-time pillar of the community. We bumped into some old friends and were introduced to the new husband of the daughter of a dear client. We hit it off from the start. Really nice guy, told us he spends his winters in Montana as a ski instructor. Like me, the Navy brought him to Pensacola eons ago and it's come in and out of his life over the past 50 years. I couldn't resist taking the conversation to my glory days as a helicopter flight instructor. He gave me my glory without hesitation or counter-volley. It was at the reception about 30 minutes later, I learned that my new friend had quite a history. A decorated fighter pilot, shot down twice over Vietnam, he later flew with the legendary Blue Angels. I was never so impressed by a person's choice to remain silent.

Alex followed the long and winding road south and came home for the Thanksgiving holiday. He arrived just after midnight on a Monday and I woke up from a couch slumber to give him a big man-hug. At the beginning of every month, Kathleen has been going through the old photo albums and putting pictures on the fridge from the corresponding month of years gone by. It's truly amazing that the silly boy on the fridge, in the superman costume, would turn into the young man before us. The recipe was relatively simple. Take the boy, add love (most of the time, the easy part), massive amounts of discipline (sometimes, not as easy), pray for divine intervention, and bake on high for 18 years. For those of you out there with younger kids or grandkids, and you're just not sure you won't be making prison visits in the future, I promise you it will work out. Everyone's on their own schedule, but if you're patient, the recipe is pretty solid if you follow it completely.

"You can't always get what you want," crooned Sir Mick, so righteously. Collin won't be attending the Coast Guard Academy. It was tough news, but after three days in the rearview mirror, the kid was taking it in stride. They let him down with an email and rather than mope and wallow in a pity party, my son immediately took to plan B and put out a couple more college applications. He received the disappointment on a Wednesday and didn't let us know about it till Saturday night, on a break during the Alabama/ Auburn game. The boy has come a long way from his picture on the fridge and has unquestionably learned from this experience. Life is hard and though you don't always get what you want, in the end, you always "get what you need." Thanks Mick.

Blackjack. Kathleen and I hit twenty-one years of wedded bliss last month. Collin is probably going to put me on that web site (inside joke), but I love her more every year. In my humble opinion, the marriage recipe is similar to the one for child-rearing. Massive quantities of love (always the easy part!), mix in discipline (marriage is a full-contact sport), and constant prayers for divine intervention. Kathleen will never let me forget the time, early on in our marriage, I made the comment, "Life sure is more complicated now." Some things are better left unsaid. This year, our anniversary fell smack dab on Turkey Day, which worked out well since the gift for 21 years is cranberry sauce. We celebrated the event by driving about an hour west to Point Clear, Alabama, for Sunday brunch at the celebrated Grand Hotel. The place holds special meaning for us because it was there, nearly 22 years ago, that I popped the question, "Would you please pass the mustard?"

In the Navy

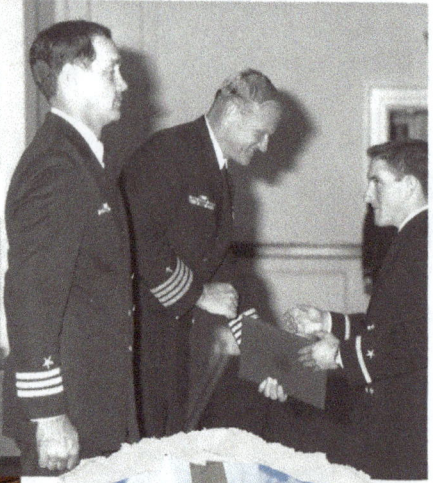

Architect?

Taking DC by storm

Homeless...

Vacation 2006

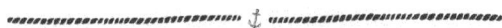

2015

January 2015

So it goes in wealth management, and life in general. And what better time to examine your present station than the beginning of a new calendar year. The first step in planning of any kind should be a thorough assessment of where you currently stand. If you're happy with your situation, your goal should be to take actions that give you the best likelihood of continuation. If you seek change, your planning should focus on the incremental steps you'll need to take to get you to your desired destination. The more drastic the change, the more incremental steps along the way. In any case it's up to you. Your future is yours for the making. Don't dally. Let the calendar light your fire and make it happen.

Wake up Little Susie. Collin beamed back in time and stole the plot from that playful ditty made famous by the Everly Brothers in 1957. We awoke on Saturday morning and found our youngest had busted his curfew and spent the night out at a friend's. See the jukebox for his excuse. Kathleen ordered him home immediately. He'd get some money and go pick up a drug test at CVS. Upon his arrival, we saw he was fine and obviously not hung over - which sadly, would have been the likely case if it were me at his age. So, we chewed him out and introduced him to that 1984 classic hit from the Pretenders, "Back on the Chain Gang." The timing was perfect, a broken foot kept me from doing some much-needed yard work and wouldn't you know… it was the best damn yard work I'd ever gotten out of the kid with nary a peep out of him. It was good to see him so understanding of the adage, do the crime, do the time.

One down and seven to go. Alex finished his first semester at Alabama and when the music stopped, he'd racked up a solid 3.83 GPA. Not a bad start after the early scare of a D on his first calculus exam. I think he's successfully re-tooled his study habits for the demands of a college engineering program. He's home now and catching up on his sleep. That is the understatement of the decade. The kid would sleep past noon if we let him. At first, I got angry and would intervene, but the more I thought about it, the more I realized that the kid costs me a lot less when he's unconscious. When he's asleep he's not eating, driving, using hot water, or electricity in any form. So now, as long as he doesn't sleep through his work schedule, I don't care if he gets bedsores!

With the Coast Guard Academy out of the picture, Collin is leaning towards the University of Central Florida as a solid Plan B. The college of business administration is his likely destination and who knows, maybe a future planner with Soundside Wealth Advisors. We ride him pretty hard, but Kathleen and I are very proud of him. He's figured out the High School thing and pulled off two "all A" grading periods in a row. The one thing that has me worried is his car. It's the one domain over which he has complete control and the last time I looked inside, it looked like a hobo-camp. That's actually a slam on hobo-camps. I'm terrified to think what his dorm room will look like if we let him go over the horizon to college. At this point, the only hope is a Felix Unger type roommate.

February 2015

Collin has been working at the Aloha Grill for over two years now. Crazy thing is, given the rampant turnover in the restaurant industry, other than the owner and his family, Collin has seniority at the place. He came home last night and griped about being blamed for a mistake that wasn't his. He could have ratted out the true culprit but it was easier to just take the hit and move on. Grumpy dad explained that when you reward bad behavior, it tends to get repeated and even though it might seem a bit jerkish, next time he might try a different tack. Well wouldn't you know, when the lad returned from work the following night, he had a new spring in his step. He decided to start acting like a "boss" and really enjoyed the experience. I see some promise in this one.

Our kids think I pick on them so here's one for them. It was the 3rd Monday of January and the financial markets were closed but I had an appointment with some new clients in Destin. I used the holiday as an excuse to dress casually so I could ride my motorcycle. As I passed through Fort Walton

Beach, I noticed an approaching procession of motorcycles, cars, and a military marching band. Fort Walton Beach is the home of the Air Force Special Operations Command at Hurlburt Field. These guys are at the pointiest end of the spear and as such, it's not uncommon to see a funeral procession. One of the most beautiful signs of respect that is fairly unique to the South is the courtesy of pulling your car over and waiting the procession to pass. It doesn't have to be a military funeral, it's just something you do and it makes me mist up to think how it must make the family members feel. So, I pulled over, took my helmet off, and stood at attention as first the motorcycles passed, then the cars, then the ROTC band. Finally, as the walking revelers approached, I realized I was paying respect to a Martin Luther King, Jr. parade!

March 2015

I can't believe that in just over six months, Kathleen and I are going to join the ranks of the empty nesters. Collin will be graduating in May and has made his college decision…envelope please…long pause…and the winner is…the University of Central Florida! Our boy called yesterday to proudly announce his acceptance to the University's Honor's College, which not only sounds pretty cool, but also gives him priority in scheduling and housing. And most importantly, he did his folks a solid in the wallet department with a couple of scholarships that, for all intents and purposes, cover his tuition. I will admit that I'm a little concerned about our free-spirited second born being eight hours over the horizon, faced with a future choice of going to class or a 45-minute drive to surfing the Atlantic, but such are the choices of the free. And the consequences have been spelled out in advance. As goes the scholarship, so goes the opportunity, so we face the future with hopeful optimism.

Have you ever had a dream career that just didn't turn out? Singer in a rock-and-roll band? Astronaut? Stand-up comedian? You got me…check, to all of the above. Unfortunately, skills and talent got in the way every time. I've got to admit I'm a little proud of one that didn't get away. Like many of you, I love to read. I've always wondered what it would be like to be on the other side, to put pen to paper and create something that could be useful or entertaining to a person or two. Well, it's definitely not entertaining, but I hope my first effort will be useful. "You're Gonna Make It: The Indispensable Guide for a Woman Facing Divorce", was published last month. I hope none of you will ever need it, but the odds are about 100% that you'll know someone who might. My goal was to create a guide for someone whose life has just exploded. I used my experience as a financial planner and certified divorce financial analyst to describe the process, the players, and the issues through the eyes of a fictional couple based on a compilation of women I'd helped over the years. Throughout the book, I placed interviews of women who have successfully navigated the hazards and are now safely and happily on the other side. It's available in electronic format on the Kindle Store, and in print format by shooting me an email. On deck is a happier project. Tentatively called, Soundings; Reflections from a dad, husband, and financial planner will be a compilation of page four of these newsletters over the years. I'm hoping it falls into the entertaining category.

May 2015

,,,

....

"A life is not important except in the impact it has on other lives"

Jack Roosevelt, aka "Jackie" Robinson

....

How do you keep score? How do you measure success or more immediately, what constitutes a good day? For some it's the size of their bank account. For others it's their status in the community. Still others, it's the impact they've made on a stranger. There's no right or wrong answer but I suggest for those nearing retirement, it's a good idea to understand yourself on that level. Chances are your career was a tremendous part of your identity and sense of worth. A healthy pre-retirement exercise is to picture your post-retirement routine and replace the lost career challenges and satisfaction with something meaningful. Jackie's quote above is not a bad place to start.

Collin had a big week that didn't end on Friday. It was the weekend of his Prom, an adventure in itself. Always the procrastinator, he made his "ask" on Monday of the week of the event. Maybe it was pity, maybe the opportunity to attend with an upperclassman, whatever the case, she accepted his invitation. Funny thing, his date was the younger sister of one of Alex's friends. Even funnier, this friend was a captain of the high school wrestling team so Collin was on his best behavior! The evening concluded without a call from the Police so in the eyes of mom and dad, it was a good prom.

June 2015

"Life is about making an impact, not making an income."
Kevin Kruse

In the span of two days, Collin turned 18 and graduated from High School. He can now vote and enlist in the Marine Corps. He's passing on the USMC for now and will be heading to Orlando in mid-August to give the University of Central Florida his best shot. With that crazy internet thing, he actually found his future dorm-mate on the school's online forum. Funny thing, he'll be rooming with the son of an old Navy friend of mine from my last tour on the USS John F. Kennedy. So far, as previously reported, his focus is on a business degree. A post-degree maritime career is not completely out of the picture, Coast Guard, or Homeland Security. We'll see how things look as time goes on. As for the voting thing, rest assured that Collin will not let that privilege go unexercised. He's endured my rantings forever and he surely knows my beatings would be merciless.

July 2015

People with unique skills tend to be well-compensated. Surgeons, nuclear engineers, undersea welders, or as my hero Napoleon Dynamite says, those with "computer-hacking skills." But I think you can take Mr. Punja's mantra one step further and make it work for nearly anyone. There will always be demand, opportunity, and upward mobility for anyone who works a little harder than the average bear. Whether white collar or blue, provided the task is still relevant in today's economy, that's ultimately the quickest way to the American Dream.

August 2015

> *"I have been impressed with the urgency of doing. Knowing is not enough; we must apply. Being willing is not enough; we must do"*
>
> Leonardo da Vinci

My mother's a ginger...red hair and freckles. My brothers and I didn't get the hair but we do share her complexion. Growing up in the days of sun-worshipping, I had some major body-image issues. I compensated with massive amounts of physical fitness and probably a smidgin' of bulimia. Fast forward to the present and the latest trend... the Dad Bod. In a piece titled, "Why Girls Love the Dad Bod", Mackenzie Pearson explains. "The dad bod is a nice balance between a beer gut and working out. The dad bod says, "I go to the gym occasionally, but I also drink heavily on the weekends and enjoy eating eight slices of pizza at a time." It turns out that women these days look at a guy that's fit and trim and see selfishness where his buddy with the paunch is more honest, natural, and potentially attentive. And they say kids have it tougher these days?!

September 2015

It started last year and will continue for two more. An odd birthday ritual for my beautiful wife, we drop off Alex at the University of Alabama every year on her special day. It was brutal last year, the first time. This year, as the boy is somewhat settled into his routine and his future becomes more clear, there was more celebration than apprehension. In fact, Kathleen's prevailing emotion was "guilt" for the fact that she didn't cry more as we pulled away. Made me realize that I actually am a man because as sensitive as I tend to be, I am orders of magnitude from that!

Now what? Kathleen and I spent a night and the next morning in Jacksonville Beach. After a nice walk in the sand, we passed an elementary school as we headed back to the hotel. A young couple crossed the street in front of us, obviously after having just dropped off a youngin' for her first day of school. The mom turned to her husband and asked the question that began this paragraph. Kathleen and

I just smiled as we had the same question a few days earlier after dropping Collin off to begin his college journey.

November 2015

"Dear Optimist, Pessimist, and Realist, while you guys were busy arguing over the glass of water, I drank it. Sincerely, the Opportunist."

Author Unknown

Just when you let yourself exhale a little, they go and kick you squarely in the jejunum. I've told you about Alex and his freshly paved road to a career in civil engineering. Well wouldn't you know the road has forked. Our first-born thinks he may be better suited for a career in finance and economics. Analytical as he is, Al is not making any rash decisions. He met with both his engineering advisor and an advisor in the business school and has selected a course load that will allow him to go in either direction at the end of his next semester. I have to admit that Kathleen and I were a bit shocked at his announcement since the kid came out of the womb with a slide-rule, but we have faith (help us God!) and confidence that the lad will weigh his options and make a thoughtful choice when push comes to shove. There go those few remaining non-gray hairs.

Collin is chugging along in Orlando. He's still a finance major, and as far as we know, his grades are trending in the right direction. His earliest class is 10:30 AM which gives him a few hours every morning to study and work out...ya' right! A few weekends ago, he packed up the station wagon and drove to St. Augustine to meet up with some old high school friends and hit the surf. The entire east coast was getting pounded by the waves from Hurricane Joaquin, so the old gang had a great time. Since he hadn't received his first check from work yet, I wondered how he swung it financially as mom and dad don't issue food stamps or finance recreation. Alas, the lad bought two loaves of bread and a jar of peanut butter, and made PBJ the main course of every meal. Calories are calories.

I made it to my first motorcycle rally. I know what you're thinking. Leather, chrome, and big-busted, scantily-clad women. Well, it wasn't a Harley rally (not that there's anything wrong with that, my Harley friends!) I mounted my old steed and rode to the annual BMW Riders Association event. To be honest, most of the folks were old retired guys. In fact, I made the trip with a friend (retired but not old), and met another friend (ditto) who was on his way back from an adventure in Montana. It was a great time. The twisty roads in northwestern Arkansas were lined with trees in all of their fall splendor. A few weeks later, tragedy struck. Friends Hank and Sharon Neal were killed while riding their big Honda on the backroads of Tennessee. Talk about a sharp blow to the solar plexus. Hank, retired law-enforcement, was one of the most situationally aware and conservative riders I knew. Sharon had just retired and had logged thousands of miles on the back of the big Goldwing. We will miss them dearly and draw 3 lessons. First, if there's someone who needs to know that you love them, there's no time like today. There's no guarantee of tomorrow. Second, please update your will and other legal documents. It will save your family a lot of heartache. Third, be grateful for the blessings of every day and if it's in your nature, give it up to the Creator, the keeper of the ultimate plan.

December 2015

"Sooner or later, those who win are those who think they can."

Richard Bach

Great quote from the author who made a hero out of a rogue seagull. Decades prior, Henry Ford, the man who crushed the buggy whip industry, made a similar observation. In either case, the quote-smith is spot on. The world is filled with massively successful people who shouldn't be. Good thing they didn't listen.

Keeping with tradition, we hosted the Thanksgiving meal this year. As the nieces and nephews start families of their own, the crowd gets smaller. We substituted some family with some friends and still managed to get to around 20 to gather round the tables. We did have an unexpected incident. One of my very favorite people in the universe was more than a little bit late to the party. Aunt Judy set out on time; her vintage Crown Victoria loaded with her signature Del Monte French-cut green bean dish. When she finally arrived nearly an hour late, the Juder was quite visibly upset. Now for the rest of the story. Since we moved to our place in 1999, our signature red mailbox was the trademark "x" that marked the spot to our home. A couple months back, a truck versus mailbox event necessitated its replacement. I opted for the deluxe, pre-painted version and chose to forgo tradition and leave its factory copper hue intact. Much to her dismay, Judy didn't get the memo and spent the good part of 45 minutes driving back and forth in search of the familiar landmark that was no more. The good news is, being a devout Catholic, Judy turned to St. Anthony, the Patron Saint of all things lost. I'm not sure it warrants miracle status, but the first driveway Judy chose was ours and the story had a happy ending.

Last week, Kathleen and I celebrated 22 years of marriage. I often tell people that my bride's only flaw is low self-esteem…that's how I landed her. There was one other little thing. She was not a motorcycle person. It started way back in childhood where her dad's old family business was selling monuments. Not hard to imagine more than a couple of sales to a family who'd lost a loved one to a motorcycle accident. Well surprise of all surprises, after a robust sales pitch from yours truly after church on an absolutely perfect day, my beautiful bride pulled on her boots, donned a black leather jacket, and with my help, strapped on a spare helmet. We took a relaxing ride on the beach road that connects Navarre to Pensacola Beach, probably one of the prettiest and most serene rides on the planet. Wouldn't you know, like Mikey from the Life cereal commercials, she liked it! I'll keep you posted but I sure hope I've started something.

Reunion long time coming

Birthday fun

Rebuilding

Goofballs

Proud

2016

January 2016

How about a couple success stories? Lance and Kaleb worked at a local rental car company. It was a landing spot until they figured out where they might fit into the world. Both soon moved on. Lance, a gregarious lad married to our niece Kimberly, a talented and successful hair stylist, heard of a sales job at a small company that made high-end shears for stylists. Caleb, called to public service, joined the Escambia County Sheriff's Office. Latest update, Lance was recently named one of the top 5 sales reps in the whole company and awarded a trip to Hawaii. Kaleb, still sporting his "new-officer-smell", was awarded the Medal of Courage for "displaying exceptional courage and selflessness in the midst of great personal danger." Ladies and gentlemen, there are lots of good ones out there.

February 2016

"Wall Street indexes have predicted nine out of the last five recessions."

Paul Samuelson

Alex's car is gone. In a way, it's almost like a long-time girl-friend...they've been through a lot together. Al bought his old Jeep with his own money, sort of. Way back when the boys were about 11 and 12, I seeded an account for each. They started with $500 each and the deal went like this. Every all-A report card would bring a deposit of $100. It dropped to $50 if a B made the mix. Additionally, anytime the lads would delay gratification and put their own money aside, I'd match it dollar-for-dollar like a supercharged 401(k). The thought was, in 4 – 5 years, they'd each have enough money for the typical "beater" a 16-year-old boy should own. To add an educational component, I invested the money in a growth oriented mutual fund. The great recession didn't do them any favors, but even so, Alex picked up his snappy and somewhat trusty steed which served him well right up until last month. It died in Pensacola and after towing it to our trusted family mechanic, we got the diagnosis the following day. It was terminal. Still mobile, big Al is down to two wheels, trekking from his apartment to campus on his 1994 Suzuki motorcycle. Where there's a will (a warm jacket, gloves, and a backpack), there's a way.

Collin is still styling in his old Saturn station wagon which he affectionately calls the "Swag Wagon". Living on campus, it sits parked most of the time unless surf is up in the Atlantic. With the first semester under his belt and scholarship intact, we've exhaled just a little bit. I've got to admit, I'm proud of the kid. He's been working at the dining hall just across from his dorm and making his mark as he tends to do. Collin's can-do attitude has always served him well. Last weekend, his boss took the time to give him a hand-written thank-you note with just such a comment. Needless to say, it was well received. Don't get me wrong, the kid may still end up in prison, but if he does, I think he'll be a cell-block leader.

March 2016

"Prosperity is not without many fears and distastes; and adversity is not without comforts and hopes"

Sir Francis Bacon

Spring Break starts next week and our first born let us know that he'll be on a mission trip during his time off. I figured it would be something like Costa Rica, doing good work in a beautiful, tropical environment, girls in bikinis... you get the picture. Not quite. He'll be spending his break in inner-city Detroit. Who IS this kid?!

By far, the most memorable event of February was a family reunion. We all know there's no such thing as a normal family. That said, the last time my brothers and I were in the same physical space with our folks, Bill Clinton was President and we'd never even heard of Monica Lewinsky. I won't get into history, let's just say that Kagans can be hard-headed, a good trait for a motorcyclist, but not as so much for resolving misunderstandings. Well, the setting was my dad's 82nd birthday and my brother Jay and I decided it was time. Brother Josh couldn't make it physically but was there in spirit. I made the drive and Jay flew down to Sarasota...which if you didn't know, is really part of New

England. I picked up Jay at the airport and we gave the folks a call. "I'm on a road-trip'" I said. "Where to?" mom asked. "Sarasota", I replied. "Holy %*#$# (or something to that effect ;), she responded. "Are you alone?" "Nope, I'm here too" said Jay, and so began what would be the first day of the rest of our lives, a newly connected family. We had a wonderful weekend; I'll spare you the details but I will say that the little hole that was in all of our hearts has since filled in. I'd also suggest that if folks as hard-headed as us Kagans can do it, there's hope for anyone.

April 2016

I hate this quote. It's such a cop out. Life is about taking chances, putting yourself out there for something important. Taking a risk, when the reward is meaningful. Remember the classic intro to ABC's Wide World of Sports? How can one truly experience the thrill of victory if they've never felt the agony of defeat? It's about believing in yourself, your cause or endeavor, and having the faith to commit, despite the possibility of failure. A little faith in the creator doesn't hurt either.

I've had lower back issues forever. Probably started in the early days of powerlifting at Pep's Gym in downtown Framingham, Massachusetts. I was always a runty kid and figured I better beef up so I could keep my lunch money. Pep's was a place right out of a Rocky movie. No fancy machines, hot tub, or even a clean shower for that matter. It was iron, concrete, and rubber mats. If I close my eyes, I can smell the combination of rust, sweat and industrial cleaner. So here I was, looking for relief from the spasms that came at ever shrinking intervals. I tried Yoga but it was a little to

"New Age" for me. Enter Pilates; Yoga without the incense. Kathleen has been a follower for years now and I know a couple manly men who swear by it so I decided to tag along with my better half to a class last month. I'm hooked. Great stuff, my back's not felt this good in years, and I'm the only dude in class. One hazard, with all that reaching, twisting, bending and stretching, I'm always on guard against an errant squeaker.

You've probably heard of fantasy football. Collin has recently picked up fantasy investing. His roommate (Hey Praveen!), a fellow finance major, stumbled upon a cool website: Investopedia.com. It's chock full of interesting information on stocks and trading. But what got these guys hooked was the stock simulator and they, along with their other roommates, are now competing for bragging rights. It's still early, but I'll let you know if the kid's got a future with Soundside.

June 2016

Working together. Wouldn't that be a nice change? Is it me or have we become a society of hyphens and initials? It's time to get off the crazy-train where everyone has a persecution complex. Kathleen and I recently attended a meet and greet for our State Representative who is running for the Florida Senate. During the Q&A session, a guest used the term African-American to which our guest-of-honor politely took exception. A man of color, he said that he was not a hyphenated American, just an American (also a West Point grad and Army veteran). He went on to say that as a country, we need to get back to our roots. All of these labels have done nothing but divide us and have actually brought us backwards as a nation. Amen to that and I can say that two votes will be headed to that candidate in November.

Thin Lizzy or the Bus Boys…"the Boys are Back in Town". Alex and Collin made their triumphant returns from college just in time to grant momma a special Mother's Day gift; an afternoon of family yard work. For an encore, they cooked dinner and even cleaned up. They scored some huge brownie points. I may even put them back in the will.

Collin finished up his freshman year at the University of Central Florida. After a 1st semester wakeup call, the lad buckled down and did what he had to do. Can you say 4.0? I'm very proud of the kid and happy to report that he's keeping good company. Two of his three roommates also earned 4.0's and the 3rd, not exactly a slacker, pulled off a 3.9. The band is staying together for their sophomore year but will be moving off campus into an apartment and picking up two more apartment mates along the way. Collin and Alex spent their first week of summer break in the gainful employment of our neighbor, with painting duty. Robert took a shining to the boys and has made a habit out of making work for them when they're home on break. As for the rest of the summer, when job searches on Pensacola Beach were unsuccessful, Collin hit pay-dirt with an internship at the Office of Criminal Conflict and Civil Regional Counsel in Pensacola. It turned out to be a great lesson in networking as the young man that recommended him was the same young man that I recommended a year back. Karma is a beautiful thing.

Alex was home for two weeks before hitting the road for his summer gig as a camp counselor. He finished up his sophomore year at Alabama. He couldn't quite pull off a 4.0 like his younger brother, but finished with a still respectable 3.8. After a lot of soul-searching, our first-born is probably going to be changing his major from engineering to accounting. Other than a reduction in his scholarship, I'm not disappointed. The world will always need accountants and I gave him the same offer that I presented his brother, a finance major. Graduate from school, pursue a career, and in 10 years, send me a resume and we'll see if we can't find a spot in the family firm.

July 2016

"One of the most tragic things I know about human nature is that all of us tend to put off living. We are all dreaming of some magical rose garden over the horizon instead of enjoying the roses that are blooming outside our windows today."

Dale Carnegie

Amen, Mr. Carnegie! Life certainly comes with no guarantees, including waking up in the morning. Besides service, gratitude is one of the sweetest elixirs and a wonderfully constructive way to begin every day is to recognize some of the many blessings in our lives. I always start with a wife that I don't deserve, kids that give me more joy than pain, a career that provides a purpose, the good fortune to be born in the U.S.A., and the awareness of a glorious God who can't keep all of the bad things that are part of this human experience from happening, but is always there to help paddle the canoe through it all.

It's been a pretty quiet summer in the Kagan household. Alex has come and gone, back up to his adopted sweet home Alabama. He got a gig as a lifeguard and camp counselor up on a lake just south of Andalusia. We don't talk much, but creeping on his Facebook page has revealed it's one of the best experiences he's ever had and he's grown considerably from it. I know the counselor role has forced him out of his comfort zone, always a good thing for a young adult. We did get to meet his "girlfriend" a few weeks back. The quotes are included because, according to our son, so far, they're just friends. This weekend is the 4th of July and he's going to meet her family, down from Colorado for vacation. I think there's more to this story.

We never see Collin. He is our nomad and pretty much lives out of his car...a bit frightening but good to know that in a pinch, or the inevitable zombie apocalypse, he will adapt. The photography bug has bitten hard and he's put a good chunk of his summer earnings into new gear including a waterproof case so he can take action surfing shots.

As for me, I made another trip out west on the motorcycle to promote my new brand, Next Adventure Wealth Advisors (nextADVwealth.com). This time, it was southwestern Utah to attend the 16th annual Red Rock Rendezvous. The total journey was about 4,200 miles and I only got rained on for a couple hours on the first leg. Around 120 ventured there from all over the map and while checking in, I met some folks from California, two of whom shared my interest in off-road exploration. I set out the following morning with a group of seven. It was a gorgeous day, the scenery was spectacular. We cruised past the red rocks of Bryce Canyon and up to Capital Reef National Park. The roads and vistas were incredible, other-worldly really. Martian red and lunar gray with alien looking rock formations. When the pavement ended, our group was whittled down to 3 of us on adventure bikes, BMW "GS" models designed to be equally comfortable cruising 80 mph on the interstates of west Texas, or crossing a stream in the backwoods of Blackwater State Forest. The highlight of the trip was the famous Burr Trail Switchback Road, the lowlight came shortly afterwards. After the switchbacks, I stopped to take a couple of pictures. I remounted and gave it some throttle to catch up with my two new riding buds. As I approached the first, we hit a washout area and the sand got a bit deeper. The forces of the universe conspired to put a car on this desolate dirt road coming from the opposite direction. The rider in front of me steered to the right to give the car more room. At the same time, the sand called for more throttle and I obliged. Freaked out by the sand, the other rider decelerated and turned left in search of firmer terra. The car prevented me from going left and we ended up sharing the same piece of universe. No injuries, but both bikes were disabled. In the middle of nowhere with no cell coverage, we sent our third man to arrange for a rescue. More than 6 hours later, just as the sun was beginning to set and unspoken thoughts of settling in for the evening filled both our heads, a truck towing a flatbed trailer appeared over the horizon.

Happy ending. We ventured 4 hours east to Grand Junction, Colorado, the nearest suitable motorcycle shop, and the next morning I troubleshot my machine, did some battlefield repairs and was able to ride back home over the next couple days. Insurance will cover damage to both bikes and we're all around for the next adventure. On a funny note, I learned what Hell is like. My partner in stranded-ness turned out to be an out-spoken liberal, man-purse wearing, vegan from San Francisco who thinks the government should regulate veganism. Good times.

We have no grandkids yet, but grand-nephews make me a Gruncle. The gang lives in Orlando but Facebook is awesome and we love videos. I don't know how it came to pass but it seems that my 4-year-old great nephew is giving me credit for teaching him all the coolest things. From cheering on his soccer team on TV in his underwear, to cool gymnastic moves on the swings in the backyard, when asked who taught him that, his response, "Uncle Jonny". I can't wait to buy him a minibike.

August 2016

"Never confuse activity with results."

Louis V. Gerstner, Jr.

I n another life, I was a Navy helicopter flight instructor. It was a three-year tour and the source of more than a few of my gray hairs. In the basic instrument stage of training, student would be "under-hood" while performing maneuvers. An example would be maintaining altitude and airspeed while executing 30° angle of bank turn to the left. The average student would let the nose drop, lose altitude and gain airspeed, two parameters that were supposed to remain constant. They'd say, "I'm low and fast" but often, in Seinfeld-ian fashion ("you can take a reservation, you just can't HOLD a reservation") they'd skip the important part where they pulled back the stick and added power to get back to the desired airspeed and altitude. Diagnosis without corrective input is not only frustrating, it does nothing to get you closer to your goals, financial or otherwise.

Alex is back but not for long. It was a successful summer up at Camp Blue Lake just south of Andalusia, Alabama. The following are his words on the experience. "As I walked up to Dogwood Cabin 4, I didn't know what to expect. It was week 2, the Middle Schoolers, and they were supposed to be terrors. I was more nervous than I had been for anything else so far during the summer. I hoped it didn't show. As the kids started to arrive, my mood changed drastically. The campers filed into the cabin and I introduced myself. It was a shock to see how respectful these middle schoolers were; the exact opposite of what I'd expected. The week flew by, as they all did. On Friday night in the camp Chapel, I was honored to serve communion to my campers. I made eye contact with each of them and called them by name as I served them. It was a very powerful moment and I could tell that they were soaking in every part of it. Once the service was over, one of my campers, John, came up to me and asked if we could talk. We stood outside of the chapel and he told me about different problems that he had going on in his life. I was shocked to hear everything that he was telling me because he was one of the happiest and most caring campers I had that week. Once he finished, his youth pastor and I prayed over him. John later told me that that moment meant so much to him, and he was so thankful that I was his counselor. He told me that I was so influential on him and he thanked me for everything I had done for him over the course of the week. Having John tell me all of this was the highlight of my summer. Looking back at my expectations at the beginning of the week I felt a bit ashamed for thinking the middle school campers were going to be bad before I ever met them. It made me realize that sometimes your greatest victories and joys will come in times and circumstances that you never expected. Never write something off because you are scared, nervous, or unsure of its outcome. It might be exactly what you need, you just don't know it yet." Doggone it kid, I'm crying again.

Collin's summer is rolling right along. Nothing as spiritually enlightening as big brother's but it would be boring to have two of the same kid. We've tried to teach our boys good financial habits and I will say that they both live within their means (they have no choice). But Collin chooses to live exactly AT his means, a problem when you are only paid once a month and the brakes in your not-so-trusty 12-year-old station wagon go out. He found out the hard way the importance of having an emergency account. The lad's car sat pitifully in the driveway while he did odd jobs around the neighborhood to scrape the money together to fix her up. Luckily, Uncle John (for the price of some Miller Lite) helped with the labor and everything worked out. Did he learn anything? I'm not sure; the balance in his bank account currently sits at $1.11. It's a hat trick, I'm crying again.

September 2016

Like beauty, talent is a wonderful thing. I wish I had a little of both. Unfortunately, they're qualities that pretty much come from luck, or as my brother-in-law says, being a member of the lucky sperm club. Grit on the other hand, is all you. We all know intelligent and talented folks who've squandered opportunities for lack of grit or perseverance. Even more sad when you wonder how many folks threw in the towel just as they were on the brink victory. I believe it's important that a business plan for any new endeavor has an exit strategy just in case. That said, patience, like grit, is often the rarest of virtues.

Once again, Kathleen and I are empty nesters. We dropped Alex off in Tuscaloosa in early August. The kid's firing on all cylinders. He's loving his business classes. After engineering, managerial accounting is a piece of cake and he still gets to use his beloved frontal lobe. Big Al is living off-campus in an apartment with three of his pals from the last couple of years. As an added bonus, his girlfriend (yes, they've gone public) lives a few units over. And, the kid has an income. We told both our sons that they're on their own for living expenses starting their junior year. We want them to get used to the ways of the world so it's not a shock upon graduation. Alex hit the job search pretty hard and ended up with a pretty cool gig. He rolled up to the farmer's market on his motorcycle and the first person he met said he'd fit in great with the other two motorcyclists employed there. During the interview, he learned that his future boss was a CPA by trade and this market was a side business to quench his penchant for farmers and farming. You might remember that Alex is in the process of changing his major to accounting so if this wasn't a sign, there's no such thing.

The night before Collin left for school, he helped me out at a seminar I held at the local motorcycle shop. "An idiot's guide to a cross country road trip" was the encore performance of a talk I gave to my Rotary club. We advertised the event to those who'd always wanted to take such a trip but needed a little push. I told stories from the road, showed pictures and played some videos. The angle was, if a goober like me can do it, what are you waiting for? We filled the house with over 50 people and a great time was had by all. Collin was my tech guy and a great assistant during the event. The best part was afterwards, my boy came up to me and said, "Dad, you were awesome." For you parents with young teens at home, it gets better.

October 2016

If you're a believer, this is never a problem. You're always found out. For those who can't wrap their heads around a higher power, try the karma route. In my humble opinion, this is one of the biggest problems of society these days, the de-God-ing of everything. At the risk of getting sued by Yoko Ono, imagine what a world it would be if just one in ten acted as if someone or something greater was watching?

We got to see Collin last month. Sort of. I certainly don't mean to challenge the weather gods but it's been another wonderful hurricane season. No action, for us anyhow. Even so, when Hurricane Hermine was forecast to churn up the surf, my big wave enthusiast planned a last-minute impulse trip back home. He knew enough not to ask for help planning what his grumpy dad would classify as a misadventure so he worked the angles on his own. I've previously chronicled the "sketchiness" of the lad's car in these pages so you know alternate transportation was needed. Bring on Greyhound. Those who've left the driving to them know their depots aren't usually in the most up and coming neighborhoods, which Collin soon found out. After parking his car at the nearest Walmart, a couple miles away, he proceeded to walk/run in the rain through the projects carrying his briefcase with laptop to the station. It was a scene from a National Lampoon movie. Once there, the adventure continued. As the last person to load a nearly full bus, it took a trip down, up, and back down the aisles before a nice man graciously moved over to share a seat. Apparently, the surf was worth it.

An exercise in contrasts, brother Alex had far different challenges. Our eldest son has gone full tilt spiritually and the change to his attitude and overall outlook are marked. Alex has always been our introspective one, focused and serious, rational almost to a fault. Since stepping up his spiritual journey, he's taken a turn to the ethereal. In his words, "I have been blessed beyond belief. My grades have improved, I've grown as a person, I have been given countless opportunities to lead and minister to others, I have an incredible girlfriend, and it just seems like all aspects of my life are falling into place." Obviously, great stuff to hear as a dad. There's always a but, in this case, I'll call it a more constructive, "and". Basked in a newfound comfort and belief that everything happens according to a plan, when Alex's girlfriend Claire decided to accept an internship to Ghana next fall semester, he took the disappointment of their separation and turned it into pride of her decision to place service ahead of her own comforts. I'm very proud of both of them and excited to see how this journey unfolds.

Finally, a story to possibly spark the interest of an enterprising grandkid out there. Our cousin-in-law was in town on a business trip and we had a great visit. Eric is the nephew of my mother-in-law, Annie. When Annie called her friend Hilda and told her she'd be stopping by with her nephew, Hilda perked up. "How old is he?" she asked. The answer, 51, was greeted with a little disappointment. "I'd hoped he was a teenager so he could fix my computer." Not to worry. When they arrived, pleasantries were exchanged, and Eric was dispatched to the "faulty" computer. Now Eric is not an IT expert by trade (or age) but his experienced troubleshooting skills got right to the issue. In the 70's, a Saturday Night Live skit uncovered the cause of the Three Mile Island nuclear plant meltdown. Of course, I'm talking about the Pepsi syndrome where an errantly spilled soft drink on the computer keyboard which controlled the main reactor was the cause of a nuclear disaster. In Hilda's case, it was not a Pepsi but a much more sinister culprit. Turns out her kitty cat ran across her keyboard. Accident? Only the cat knows for sure. The problem trouble-shot, damage fixed, but I'm looking at that cat for questioning. As for the business opportunity, if I were an enterprising teenager with a modicum of computer skills, I'd market myself as Grandkid for Hire, Computer Services.

November 2016

"You know everyone is ignorant, only on different subjects."
Will Rogers

A twist on the above is, We're all experts, just at different stuff. It's what makes an economy. When we're starting out, one of our biggest challenges is to decide what "to be." I don't want to be that preachy guy, but I love the message from the leader of our place of worship. It's about, "Loving God, loving your neighbor and finding your place in the Greater Story." When you really boil it all down, that's a pretty good prescription for a happy and successful life, don't you think? It also should help take the edge out of that whole "what to be" issue. As long as we're moving forward and keeping the first two in mind, the rest will present itself along the way.

The US Army's newest weapon is called Noah. It's not an acronym, he's our nephew who recently graduated from basic training and jump school and is now officially a United States Army Infantryman. We're so proud of this young man. My brother Jay and his wife Joanie have raised 3 outstanding boys. Noah is their middle son. He had options. Mom and dad had been socking away money into a college fund. On his own, Noah decided to take a path of service. A nation in decline? I don't think so.

Alex turned 21 last month. I know. Kathleen looks way too young to have a 21-year-old son, but remember, we lived in Kentucky for 3 years. We got to see our newly emancipated man last weekend when he came home for fall break. He brought his girlfriend, Claire, and a few friends. They had a great time and Alex really enjoyed showing them all the place that he was so lucky to spend his formative years. They had a truly meaningful encounter while walking downtown Pensacola. Visiting the Missing Child Memorial, they met Bruce, a 57-year-old homeless man. Bruce was a Navy veteran and he shared his story. They ended up talking for an hour and afterwards, said a prayer for their new friend. The following morning was a Sunday and our son and his clan hit the beach for a church service at Flounders...gotta love the Gulf Coast! They were happily surprised to see Bruce among the worshippers. He told them that he had found the prettiest shell he had ever seen on the beach the day before. He took it out of his pocket and gave it to them. Even in his hard times, he did not fail to see the beauty in life. As you'd expect, our son and his friends were deeply moved. A nation in decline? I don't think so.

Meanwhile, Collin was living life on the edge. A practicing "starving student". With his bank account in the single digits, he dropped a resume and application off at the apartment complex where he resides after learning they were hiring leasing ambassadors. It was a great opportunity, not lost on the general population, and more than 150 like-minded twenty-somethings did the same. Collin looks pretty good on paper and was chosen as one of 30 to get a group interview. Turns out, he's pretty good in person too, and was brought back for a one-on-one interview. Three agonizing days later, he got the phone call and a job offer...one of only two selected. Needless to say, the boy was very excited and it was a huge boost to his self-esteem. Even better, he's really enjoying the job, and paycheck.

I think everyone needs a hobby. Something to do when you're not working that really gets your happy-juices flowing. Gardening, jogging, an artistic pursuit, motorcycling. Last month was the 8th annual Turkey Trot. Named for that holiday at the end of November when the event was originally held, it's a weekend camping and motorcycle ride-in up in the Blackwater State Forest. All ages and vocations are represented, united by the irrepressible addiction to explore the woods on two wheels at a speed just fast enough to produce the necessary hormonal rush that we adrenalin junkies can't live without. Around the campfire you can find young and old. There was an engineer, a surgeon, a military pilot, a student, business owners, retirees, a union rep, and even a financial planner. A veritable economy. This year's event went on without a hitch, or complaint for that matter, from more than 100 riders who came from all over the state. The riding was fantastic. Blackwater State Forest is a true gem. Used by hikers, hunters, campers, horse riders, motorcyclists, if you've never been there, google Hurricane Lake Florida. We were even treated to a Saturday morning with temperatures in the upper 30's, as refreshing as a big box of Junior Mints. Can't wait for next year, and I didn't. Went back the following Saturday for a ride with a few friends.

Pals

Fun in the dirt

Christmas 2010

Cousins

College dayz

2017

January 2017

"If your actions inspire others to dream more, learn more, do more and become more, you are a leader"

Dolly Parton

We got to see a bit of the boys during the holidays. Alex made it home first, Collin worked for nearly a week after his last final, delaying his triumphant return. As for work, Alex reached out to his former boss at the Aloha Grill and jumped right back onto the schedule. Alex is a bit of an introvert. He could have snagged a glamour spot out in the dining room as a waiter, but preferred the low-key life of a dishwasher. Upon returning from his first day back from behind the sink, he proudly related how it all came right back to him. I let him know how supremely proud I was as I thought to myself, this a what happens when every kid on the team gets a trophy.

As for college jobs, Collin is a "Community Ambassador" at the apartment complex in which he resides. His role is varied but the most useful aspect from a life-skills training standpoint is being the point person for all the questions and concerns of residents and their parents. He's discovered that many of the parents he speaks with aren't that pleased they have to speak with him in the first place. But here's where our self-described hypersensitive son has learned to use his powers for the greater good. He's decided not to take things personally. Maybe the caller had a recent crummy customer service experience, maybe their Whataburger drive-thru order was incorrect. In any case, our son has issued an ongoing personal challenge. When picking up the phone and introducing himself, it's his goal to leave the person on the other end, hanging up with a smile. Turns out, says the lad, it ends up bettering his mood as well. Who IS this kid?

February 2017

∕∕∕∕∕∕∕∕∕∕∕∕∕∕∕∕∕∕∕∕∕∕∕∕∕∕∕∕∕∕∕∕∕∕∕∕∕∕∕

"There are no secrets to success. It is the result of preparation, hard work, and learning from failure."

Colin Powell

The only people who never fail are those who never try. Life is a full-contact sport and success is usually directly proportional to the amount of scar tissue one is sporting. That said, the sweetest victories come from the toughest fights as do many of the most meaningful lessons learned. I think that's known as wisdom, or as the kid's say, old man muscles.

Prior to a trip home, Collin asked me to put him on my calendar. "Let's camp out and then ride dirt-bikes in the morning." An offer I certainly couldn't refuse. With our boys off at school, it's a rare treat to get some quality one-on-one time these days. The weather changed our plans slightly, unpredictability always adds to an adventure. We set off for Hurricane Lake Friday afternoon, got in a ride through the wet and muddy woods, set camp, then met mom and Alex for dinner at a little place right out of a John Cougar Mellencamp song up in Baker. The best part came afterwards, back at camp. Collin took the lead on the fire, a skill he surprised me with. Once blazing, we got down to the best part of the trip. Hanging out, sharing stories of the earlier ride, philosophies on life, what the future might hold, and other great stuff that makes up all that's wonderful about being a dad. There may have been a beer or two involved, I'm not telling.

At the fireside, we talked about the rocky relationship I've had with my own dad that I've shared with you all over the years in these pages. The good news is we are at a high point. We're communicating more than I can ever remember. A casualty of the rocky relationship of the past was that my own sons had never met their grandfather, my dad. By the fire, we decided that was going to change. I had a conference in Jacksonville the following weekend. Collin lives in Orlando attending the University of Central Florida. We decided on a Sunday rendezvous in Sarasota, the home of my folks. Again, beer may have been involved.

Over the next couple of days, I was excited, but at the same time, a little terrified. Rather than risk being denied an audience, we'd take the gamble and just show up. I know, gutsy move. What if our reception was less than enthusiastic? I did not share this part with my son, who was nothing but excited. He'd never met my dad but heard all the stories. In Collin's words, "mostly exaggerated pity stories to make me and my brother not take things for granted." Dad, can we get McDonald's?, would be answered with, "When I was a kid, we'd get mush for breakfast, lunch and dinner.. and we liked it!" So how did it go? I'll let Collin tell you. "Meeting him went better than I could have dreamed. We sat around the table for a few amazing hours making up for the time we had missed. I could not stop smiling the entire night, he reminded me of my father so much: from the corny jokes, to the showtime personality, even his laugh was a reflection of my dad's. We left that night with full stomachs and full hearts, but I couldn't help but think about how similar the two of them were. It was sobering to think of any situation where I did not have my dad to bounce my problems off, talk to, or beg for money for my books for school. So in this short time I had with my grandfather, he did share his stories and pass along his insights, just as I had seen my other friends grandfathers do for them. However, his biggest impact was having me realize how lucky I was to have the relationship I do have with my family, and to never take time you have with anyone for granted."

I turned my back and our eldest son Alex had become a man. A junior, studying accounting at the University of Alabama, he's learned about the importance of networking. He put this to practice recently at an event hosted by the accounting school called 'Meet the Firms'. They bring in representatives from 35 accounting firms and hold a mixer with the students at the most motivational of venues, Bryant-Denny Stadium, home of the legendary Crimson Tide. Alex had a great night, made strong connections with 7 firms, and was told to stay in touch to set up internships in the future.

Even better, the event motivated Alex to crank things up a notch and make a more personal connection. After a guest lecturer made an interesting presentation, Alex reached out and asked if he would be willing to meet and talk about his career one-on-one. The invitation was received enthusiastically and the two met for dinner the following week. It was a fantastic meeting; Alex found several points in common and they immediately connected. From their faith, to their past pursuits of engineering, Alex's effort outside the classroom was arguably the best lesson he's received to date. He'd made a contact, a friend, and a professional advocate, some of the most powerful things a student can acquire. He's going to need them. His bedroom is about to be my new office.

March 2017

"The road to success is not easy to navigate, but with hard work, drive and passion, it's possible to achieve the American dream."

Tommy Hilfiger

The son of a watchmaker, Hilfiger was raised in upstate New York. He had a happy childhood as the second of nine children…a good Catholic family. He credits his parents for his solid work ethic. After spending the summer of his 18th year working in a clothing store in Cape Cod, he took his $150 life savings and opened his own clothing store in 1971. Fast forward to 2006, when he sold Tommy Hilfiger for $1.6 billion, Mr. Hilfiger continues to live the American dream. To anyone who feels that dream is dead, reread the above quote above or better yet, Hilfiger's memoir, "American Dreamer", a NY Times bestseller published last year.

My cell phone rang during the first quarter of the Super Bowl. Now I'm a New England fan so I was not particularly in the mood for idle chit chat but our son was so excited. No, he's not a Falcon's fan, he wasn't even watching the game. He was at a baptism. Last summer, our first-born worked at Camp 1831. Run by the University of Alabama, it's for incoming freshmen and transfer students to help them adjust to college life while also learning how to become leaders from their peers. Alex was in charge of a group of 15. I've noted previously that our first-born is inclined to be the strong, silent type. This role took him squarely out of his comfort zone, a place where our most meaningful impact is usually born. Alex noticed that one of his students, Brandon, was having a growth-moment of his own. He decided to take Brandon under his wing with some positive mentorship. It was very well received. They built a relationship that continued as the semester began. It turned out that as a result of Alex's mentorship, Brandon also became passionate to serve. Alex gave him the confidence to pursue those passions. Two of his outlets…student government and his faith. Back to the Baptism. When Alex learned that Brandon was to be baptized on Super Bowl Sunday, he knew that was an event he would not miss. He arrived unannounced and when Brandon saw him after the ceremony, he said there were a couple folks he wanted Alex to meet…his parents. When introduced, Brandon's mom took my son's hands in her own and told him how thankful she was for everything he'd done for her son. She said that every mom hopes and prays that their child will find someone that will help build them up and make them a stronger person and Alex was that person. My boy walked away from that conversation with tears in his eyes. He was a junior at a university but this was the most powerful lesson he'd learned to date. That he could make a substantial difference in someone else's life, and he realized how thankful he was for the opportunity.

As usual, 580 miles to the southeast, Collin had an interesting month. At work, he was summoned to the office by the operations and property managers. Possessing the same paranoia gene as his old man, he assumed the worst. "Don't worry, you aren't in THAT much trouble" his manager mercifully stated as my boy entered the room. He was then told that there'd be some changes in the office. Managers were being promoted, some roles realigned, and they wanted to give our young finance major some added responsibilities. He'd be putting some of his coursework to practical use as one of two new book-keepers for the apartment complex. He'll work with all the components that make up the financial statements of the property, from the budgets to balance sheet, which is exactly what he's currently doing in his accounting class at the university. The lad is very excited about his role and responsibility and the fact that it comes with a 25% reduction in his rent is just icing on the cake. A huge bonus as daddy welfare is reduced next year.

April 2017

"You only have to do a very few things right in your life so long as you don't do too many things wrong"

Warren Buffett

Alex brought his girlfriend home for the break so he was busy. We do love Claire and hope he can hang onto her. To that note, a week later, Alex and Claire flew out to Colorado to celebrate Claire's grandfather's 80th birthday with the extended family (Grandma provided Alex's ticket so they could all meet the lad they'd been hearing so much about.) Understandably, the kid was more than a little nervous. This was a big deal. "Grampy" was the family patriarch; a Navy veteran with strong political views and a deep love for his family. He played a huge part in Claire's life, was a tough judge of character, and to date, had never approved of Claire's previous boyfriends. The celebration was at the Four Season and everyone dressed for the part. With everything on the line, awash in emotions, Alex's fears were washed away as Grampy opened their conversation with joke after joke about the Navy. Years of my tall tales put

Alex in perfect position and he did great. After dinner, he overheard Grampy tell Claire, "Alex is a dude, not a dud", a clear sign he passed muster.

June 2017

Last month, Jonny went to Utah. I did not see Frankie on his way to Hollywood but it was an excellent trip none-the-less. My excuse and ultimate destination was the 2017 BMW Motorcycle Owners of America International Rally outside of Salt Lake City. Unlike last year in Hamburg, NY, the absolute certainty of day-after-day 100 + degree temperatures kept Kathleen at home. You all know how much I love my wife, but this was permission to really rough it and I took full advantage of the opportunity. I put in some grueling hours on the saddle, did a ton of moto-camping, and in the interest of time spent the bare minimum of effort on personal hygiene. It was an absolute blast.

The weekend following my return was just as special. Of course, it was wonderful to see Kathleen (after a long, hot shower and shave!) but I got the added bonus of a reunion with my all-time hero, Bob Bell, who'd just returned from a 13-month adventure of his own. Bob is currently a Professor of Business at St John's University in Minnesota, but it was just over 25 years ago that he, then a student at St. John's, was injured. While rough-housing with a dorm mate during his freshman year, he heard 2 loud pops. On the ground, no feeling in his lower body, he uttered three brief commands, "Call 911, Don't touch me, I forgive you." Bob wrote his first book, "Un-Moving Four-Ward", in 2014. It is a must read. You will laugh, you might cry, and you will never, ever again ask the question, "Why me?" Bob just returned from his sabbatical where he and his two caregivers, Hannah and Piper, spent more than a year visiting Benedictine monasteries around the world (primarily in Africa and India) helping to inspire and minister to disabled children. His next book will chronicle the experience and, if I were a betting man, offer tips on how to be a better human being. Bob is the complete package...great sense of humor, incredibly engaging manner, and of course he's easy to look at...he shares those genes of my wife's family.

One of the best parts of our reunion was the fact that both of our boys were home to chat with this international man of mystery who just happens to counsel young undergraduate business students for a living...coincidence? I just sat back and listened while Bob spoke with our boys, one-on-one, gently querying them on their thoughts, goals and plans upon graduation. First up was Alex, our accounting major. It just so happened that Bob's undergraduate degree was in accounting and his first job was with, then "Big Eight" firm, Arthur Anderson. Alex will graduate next May and is already lining up interviews mostly with regional firms. He'd never really thought about working for any of the now, "Big Four" firms. The gears they are a turning.

Next up was Collin, a junior finance major. Well wouldn't you know, after Bob tired of accounting, he went to law school and landed a job on Wall Street where he spent the next five years in the finance capital of the world. A surfer, Collin had never given much thought to life in the big city but there are a lot of things he'd never given much thought to. Can you hear the gears?!

September 2017.

"Sometimes the smallest step in the right direction ends up being the biggest step of your life. Tip toe, if you must, but take the step."

Naeem Callaway

It was the summer of 1999. I was home for lunch, living the life of a pharmaceutical rep, educating physicians on the benefits of my line of cardiovascular meds. I'm a pretty good teacher but a real crappy salesman so I was growing tired of my chosen career. The financial markets had been on a decade-long tear, CNBC was on the tube, and a commercial for a financial firm came on with the tag line, "the Greatest Risk is Not Taking One. I resigned the following day and began my current career. It was a huge step, fraught with challenges. I couldn't have known at the time, but I thank the Lord every day for giving me the push that I needed. I pay it forward whenever the opportunity presents. Don't be afraid to do the same, especially with those you love.

When it comes to life, I hate to exhale. You know what I mean. To let your guard down and get cocky with the forces of the universe that are always out there forcing us to do more and get better. That said, if everything works out, a year from now Kagan, Inc. will have one less on payroll. Alex is a senior. I exhaled a few years back. He was an engineering student with a full (engineering) scholarship at Alabama and an internship with a global engineering firm, secured during the summer after his freshman year. Done with that one right...wrong. Turned out the kid didn't really enjoy his chosen field and after much thought, prayer, and planning, decided accounting was the road he'd travel. Fast forward to the present. It looks like he just might pull it off. A full summer of classes got him on track to graduate with his class and wouldn't you know, he just accepted an internship with a large, local accounting firm, Jamison Money Farmer. They were one of several Alex had interviewed with and by far, his top choice. JMF has been around for nearly 100 years but rather than being stodgy and old (no offense to all my stodgy old compatriots out there ;), their website takes the time to tout a culture of work-life balance, where employees are treated like family. He'll be working as both a tax and audit intern, in the height of tax season...a baptism by fire. The kid is on cloud nine and naturally, so are we. But no, I haven't exhaled.

It's starting to get real for #2 son Collin, who just began his junior year at the University of Central Florida. A summer class finished up his prerequisites and he was officially accepted into the College of Business with a Finance specialty. Eons back, a business student myself at the University of Massachusetts, it was more "business-light" for me, with a focus on marketing. There will be none of that for our boy. With classes like Intermediate Corporate Finance, Equity and Capital Markets, International Business, and Supply Chain Management, this kid's gonna be ready to take the helm of Goldman Sachs, or maybe even Soundside Wealth Advisors someday. Now college is great fun, but I don't want our kids back after graduation, so they are starving students by design. Their lifestyle needs are all self-funded (eating is a lifestyle need, right?). Call it our attempt at teaching them the work-life balance. Collin tends to fly right up to the edge of the sound barrier at times but so far, he's pulling it off balancing a robust social calendar with a solid work-ethic.

Always the under-achiever (kidding), Alex's girlfriend Claire is currently in Ghana on a three-month internship in order to complete her degree in Social Work. She is working for an organization called City of Refuge Ministries at a home for children who have been rescued from the local slave trade and single mothers learning trades to become financially stable. Light stuff. I've told you in the past how much we love Claire and to date, she shares my wife Kathleen's only flaw…an obvious lack of self-esteem, judgement, and awareness of how much better she could do in the area of partner selection.

In keeping with this month's career-theme, I've got to brag on my nephews from the north a little. Brother Jay and his wife Joanie did something right. Their eldest son, Benjamin is a senior at the University of Vermont. A chemistry major, this future doctor has spent the last two summers as an intern at the Los Alamos National Lab doing some really cool and very secret stuff. I don't think it involved aliens but then again, he wouldn't say. What isn't a secret is that the genius got published. He's listed second on a study published in the journal, Royal Society of Chemistry, titled, Revisiting the bis(dimethylamido) metallocene complexes of thorium and uranium: improved syntheses, structure, spectroscopy, and redox energetics of $(C5Me5)2An(NMe2)2$ $(An = Th, U)$†. A real tear-jerker. Not to be outdone, his younger brother Noah graduated from high school in May of 2016. A couple months later, he was in Army boot camp, followed by jump school at Fort Benning. After graduation, this newly minted airborne soldier, checked into his first duty station at Fort Bliss, TX. With his unit in the field, Private Kagan had plenty of time to think about the future. His original plan was to satisfy his enlistment requirement and then use his GI Bill benefits to go to college. Solid plan, but wait a second, this kid is Airborne, that sounds a little too dull and conventional. A few weeks later, Noah sent in his application to West Point. Last night he saw his football team beat Fordham 64-6. Go Army, beat…anyone but Navy!

October 2017

Legendary investor, Templeton was also a world class contrarian. "Bull markets are born on pessimism, grown on skepticism, mature on optimism and die on euphoria. The time of maximum pessimism is the best time to buy, and the time of maximum optimism is the best time to sell." As for goals, his quote of the month is a doozy. When it comes to our kids, I'd love it if they grew up and did something to make the world a better place. At a minimum, if Kathleen and I have done our job, at the very least they won't make it worse. As for ourselves, there's nothing wrong with baby steps. Pay a compliment to the grocery store checkout clerk; give a warm smile to the toll collector; pick up a piece of trash in the parking lot. Easy stuff, no cost, and with any luck it's contagious.

When it comes to communications, our son Alex is a classic millennial. Short text-like bursts. Just the facts, ma'am. "My computer isn't working" typed our son. To be fair, it was a text, but am I wrong to want a little meat with those potatoes? I almost typed back, "My butt itches" but checked myself and instead shot back a staccato reply of my own. "Troubleshoot". The point being, you're a month away from turning 22, figure it out. A couple more volleys of text and our son got the message that I wanted him to own "his" problem. He did. The next morning, he let me know (via a text of course) that he'd got'r done and it didn't cost him, or more importantly, me, any money.

Collin is dating a movie star. You've probably seen her on the silver screen. Heck, she's so talented, she's even done cartoons. We'll have to wait for his memoirs for the scoop but in the meantime, our youngest son is living the dream. His new girlfriend pays her rent with Disney bucks, strutting around the park in a rodent suit. Yes, Collin is dating Minnie Mouse. But it's not all red carpet and celebrity parties for our second born. He's busting a move in school as well and let us know that he may graduate a semester early. I guess he's eager to get out in the world and bring home the bacon... make that cheese.

December 2017

Thanksgiving is a special time for us. Besides the obvious, it's also our wedding anniversary and this year marked number 24. Our celebration was low key. I gave Kathleen a pair of earrings that she bought for me to give to her for the occasion...God, I love that woman! Myself, I bought a fitness band and called it an anniversary present. What's more romantic than, "Honey, you're starting to overfill those t-shirts, get off your ass and do your steps." As for turkey day, we typically have the extended family over for a nice, laid-back celebration. Time marches on and most of the nieces and nephews have grown up and started families of their own, so our head count was down considerably. Our boys were both home from school and Alex brought his girlfriend Claire who had just returned from an internship in Africa. I know we're not supposed to have favorites but we're all tight here, right? Without a doubt, my favorite guest was our newest grand-niece, Ellie. Ellie is not quite nine months old and the daughter of our niece Sarah. Sarah is a wonderful person and a fantastic single-mother. The father of little Ellie, not so much. When we first learned that Sarah would be having a baby, I have to be honest, I was a little sad knowing that this little human would grow up without the benefit of a traditional two-parent household. My opinion could not be any different now. Ellie is the sweetest, happiest, most outwardly aware baby I've ever seen. I know it's early but I'm a pretty good judge of character... this kid's going do something big. And I know she could not be any more loved by her mom and the rest of her extended family. Isn't it something when a 53-year-old (fart) can learn a lesson from a toddler?

Love this woman

Happy place

New Year with the crew

Parent's weekend

2018

January 2018

G o Army! Funny thing for a former Navy Helo-Bubba to say but as I sat in the stands of AT&T Stadium on a cold and snowy afternoon in Philadelphia, I found myself on the Army side of things. It was the 118th showdown between the Army Black Knights and the Navy Midshipmen. Our nephew Noah is a plebe at West Point and his pop, my brother Jay, invited me to the iconic game when his wife's ticket became available. Big game aside, there was no way I was going to turn down an opportunity to see my nephews. Noah was accepted to West Point after just completing his enlisted basic training and follow-on jump school at Fort Benning. Of course, he's killing it and loving every minute, with just the right amount of confidence and military bearing. He was so busy and was with his girlfriend Kathleen, also a plebe, so our visit was a very limited, "Cats in the Cradle" type affair. Peter is my brother's youngest and I hadn't seen that little fella in about 6 years. Nothing little about Petey anymore. A gene on mom's side has broken him from the Kagan mold and it was comforting to have the lad along on the subway ride... just in case. He's large in stature but has the gentlest soul, and it was a blast to mess with him for a couple days and get his perspective on life in general. To the game. Wow... If you didn't see it, it all came down to the last play. With Army up by one, Navy missed what would have been the game winning field goal. Helm Yeah? Maybe next year.

Another year, another Christmas party at my favorite mother-in-law's. Annie's Christmas party is a tradition involving dinner and the exchange of gag gifts. She draws a crowd of about 20 or so of the extended family spread over four generations. The youngest was newborn, Smith Nelson; the senior, the matriarch herself. It's a Christmas party so watching the great-grandkids open presents is a highlight. But here's my one beef with the holiday in general...the "over-toying" of our youth. I know I'm a grumpy old bastard but doggone it, kids get a lot of gifts. So many, that none are really special. And God forbid they get a book, the veritable underwear of the toys-are-us generation. In my opinion, that's where the Hanukkah of my youth had a leg up. One night, one gift. Okay, sorry about that...soap box is stowed. The final act of the night is a take-your-eye-out-be-damned contest that always involves a flying projectile of some sort. This year, Annie bought two big bags of giant cotton snowballs. Can you guess how we worked off dinner? I never knew Annie had such a brutal fastball.

February 2018

"Good plans shape good decisions. That's why good planning helps to make elusive dreams come true."

Lester R. Bittel

Financial Independence. It's a simple recipe with just two ingredients…time and discipline. Like Forrest Gump's big brother said, "Time happens," it's the discipline part that often gets in the way. We want it all and we want it now. Unfortunately, it rarely works that way. When I sit with a new client and talk about their retirement lifestyle and whether their plan "works", I tell them it always works…the numbers are the numbers. The problem is, they might not add up to the lifestyle they were hoping for. Given a sufficient time horizon, I'd argue that there's no one who can't have their desired retirement lifestyle. I've had the honor lately, of meeting with several of my clients' young adult children. There's little I enjoy more than seeing the light come on when they get it.

Kids these days (or is it the parents) are so soft. I remember walking to school on any given frigid winter morning (probably had to share a pair of shoes with my little brother) stopping to warm our freezing hands in the carbon-dioxide filled exhaust of cars warming up on the side of the street. A couple weeks back, schools were closed because of the cold. Kathleen even got the day off as all of the major bridges were closed. So, what did my neat-freak do with her cherished bonus day? Who guessed clean out the cupboards? She made a game out of finding the most expired food product. Now there's an idea for a reality show. The winner - a box of corn starch. Expiration date - July 5, 2007. Not a whole lot of baking at the Kagan house.

On a recent date night, I took my bride to dinner and a movie at the local motorcycle shop. It's a function they hold about quarterly to get folks into the joint. Great time, excellent food and fellowship. For this event, it was home-made chili on a very cold night, made even better with the addition of some hearty German beer. Note to self... in the future, don't bring wife (and newly excited riding partner) to a motorcycle flick where the main theme is how dangerous they are and highlights numerous nice young family-men who made the ultimate sacrifice. Question. Is there a good Disney movie about a husband and wife riding the world together, visiting shoe stores and coffee houses every 45 minutes or so? I need it quick.

March 2018

"Fear is a reaction. Courage is a decision."

Winston Churchill

As a former pharmaceutical rep, I know that we are but the sum of our chemical reactions. Regarding fear - cortisol, adrenaline, and glucose came up in my Google search. Chemistry is pretty powerful...ask Walter White. To Churchill, courage is good. Blind faith, not-so-much. When it comes to investment management, that's where process comes in. An objective decision-making process that takes the very worst decision-making tool, chemically driven emotions, out of the picture, is crucial. By the way, the second worst...politics.

Alex came home a couple weeks back and made a special trip to a certain local hardware store. More on that next month. I finally got our eldest son to chase me out in the woods on a dirt bike. It was a blast for us both and it was nice to catch up on the hour ride to and from our unload spot way up in the north country. It had been more than a year since Alex had done any off-road riding. For the non-initiated, it is a heck of a workout and we were really ripping. A father and his first-born son have a special relationship and, weird Freudian stuff aside, it involves competition. I vividly remember playing a game of catch with my pop (our special bonding activity) on the hottest summer day. We'd take it way past the point of fun where we'd both want to quit, but neither would admit they were hot and tired and ready to hit the couch. I would invariably have to throw in the towel and give my pop the satisfaction of outlasting his offspring. Fast forward to 2018, after several hours in the woods with my boy, when Alex told me he was really starting to get a little tuckered. The needle dropped on everyone's favorite Harry Chapin single.

It's not getting any press and my evidence is admittedly anecdotal, but I will predict the career with the biggest growth potential in the next decade or two...auto mechanic. Our millennials do not have a clue how a car works. They couldn't tell an engine from a transmission from a chicken wing. Collin called me one afternoon in full freak-out mode. He had gone to watch the launch of the latest Space-X rocket (pretty cool) and on his drive back to Orlando, in a massive line of traffic, his car quit while he was in the middle of a busy intersection. Okay, it didn't actually quit. He executed an emergency shut down after a split-second diagnosis of "smoke" in the cockpit. He was in a complete panic, nearly hyperventilating and babbling incoherently. The sympathetic father I am, I gently counselled him, "SLAP YOURSELF... STOP TALKING...BREATHE..." Through further counsel and deliberate trouble-shooting, we figured out his trusty steed had a busted radiator hose and the "smoke" was the steam from the hot coolant seeking lower pressure. Good news is the trusty Saturn Wagon remains on duty.

April 2018

Often, when trying to "help" those we love, we do them a major dis-service. It's tough to see our kids struggling with an issue or challenge that we've faced in the past. It's easy to step in and take their stress away. But there's no learning in that and danger that when a challenge or pressure presents in the future and God forbid, we're not around, their path is even more difficult. As America's 2nd first lady suggested above, in love (as in investing) it often pays to think long term.

Kathleen and I have a new (future) daughter. First, some history. Joan and Jerry Kagan had three sons. I was the first, followed by Jay and Joshua. Kathleen bore us a pair of male offspring. Jay and Joanie had three sons of their own. Joshua and Krys brought another two boys to the world. See the pattern? Well, Good Friday was even better this year as Claire Carpenter answered, in the affirmative, the big question posed to her on bended knee from our first-born son, Alex.

As reality sinks in, the world feels so different. In past missives, I've written of Claire. We loved her from the start, everyone does. Kathleen and I made the trip to Tuscaloosa to be a part of the immediate post-proposal weekend and we got to meet Claire's family who flew in for the event. A young woman like Claire does not usually come by chance, so we were not surprised by how wonderful both her parents Daniel and Cynthia, and younger sister Katharine, were to be around. Everything felt right amongst the majestic old live oaks, draped in Spanish moss, as the sun began to set in that serene park along the banks of the Black Warrior River.

Now the fun really starts. Alex and Claire will graduate from the University of Alabama by the time you receive the next Soundings. Claire has already accepted a spot at NYU's Master of Social Work program this coming August and Alex is actively (to say the least) seeking meaningful employment in the Big Apple. The good news is thanks to clean living, a solid academic record, great connections (thanks Jorge Nagel and Cynthia Carpenter), and a newfound confidence coupled with an acute sense of urgency, the kid's working at least a half-dozen potential tracks. My money is on the table that he'll have a choice of offers.

As part of the process, the "kids" took a trip up to the city that never sleeps during their spring break. Among the whirl-wind of activities, Alex had several interviews, they visited the campus of NYU, and scouted out some potential areas they might lay their heads in the future. As you'd expect, money will be tight and the digs affordable to a young couple starting out their new lives will be spartan.

Their likely pad will be in the neighborhood of 400 square feet and you'll have to go out in the hall to change your mind. That said, what an adventure! Stay tuned.

May 2018

It's military appreciation month. When you add up the hours on the job it becomes pretty clear that those who serve our country aren't in it for the money. Often overlooked, the military spouse is no slouch. Taking point on the home-front can be nearly as hazardous as the front-line (one word: teenagers). If the opportunity presents, take a minute to show some love.

The Kagan family has given the frenetic markets a run for their money. The Alex show remains on center stage. We'll be heading north in a few days to see the lad graduate from college. At least we don't FEEL old. He and fiancé Claire will fly back to the Big Apple the following week where job #1 is to find job #1. He's got four interviews lined up so things are looking pretty good. Just to add a little spice, it looks like there's going to be a wedding on October 20th. I left you last month with news of the proposal. Well, the only surprise to Claire was the day of the ask. She had been busy planning for weeks. On our way home from that visit to Tuscaloosa, we got an email from our future daughter in law with a tentative guest list. It's okay, she wears the pants well.

Finally, a quick shout out to the internet. It was Saturday morning and Kathleen was doing the laundry (thanks honey!) She called me over to look at the old washing machine which had stopped running in mid cycle. At 13 years, I guess the old Kenmore gave us a good run. Just for fun, I decided to try google. Two videos later, the machine is working and $13 part is on the way which should get us decades of future loads. Russian hackers aside, I think the internet is here to stay. New problem. Who gets the Kenmore in our will?

June 2018

~~~~~~~~~~~~~~~~~~~~~~~~~~~~~~~~~~~~~~

"Prior to Capitalism, the way people amassed great wealth was by looting, plundering and enslaving their fellow man. Capitalism made it possible to become wealthy by serving your fellow man."

Prof. Walter E. Williams

It seems like only yesterday that the 3 of us (me, Kathleen, and Collin) drove tearfully away from the parking lot at Publix, with Alex in the rearview mirror (his eyes as moist as ours). We'd dropped off our boy for the first time, at the University of Alabama, our first step in shoving him from the nest. Four years later, we found ourselves sitting together with his fiancé and her extended family. Alex was graduating with honors and a degree in accounting, awaiting word from a score of interviews that would set the stage for the next act in his adventure. It was a wonderful weekend, with the perfect company. To Alex and his pursuit of employment, great news. He got an offer from his #1 pick and will begin his career with big four accounting firm KPMG this fall working in their Park Avenue complex in the heart of NYC. With that and a wedding on the horizon between now and October, the boy's got some planning to do. I'm not concerned.

We got to see Collin, briefly, at Alex's graduation, but then he was back to Orlando. You know he's a finance major at the University of Central Florida, but he's also spent the past few years working in real estate, at the complex he calls home. The pay is solid and the benefits even better which include a significant discount on his lease. But he learned the fickle nature of corporate America after the complex was sold to a new management company. With an anxious heart, he steeled himself for a meeting with the new management team. As is usually the case, his fear was misplaced. The lad walked away from the meeting with a new title, new responsibilities, a nice pay raise, and a suggestion that he give some consideration to a career in real estate management upon graduation. As our boy so adroitly put it, "You have to roll with the punches you are given, and thankfully this punch was more like a fist-bump!"

July 2018

G ood advice from Ms. Cameron; author, artist, film-maker, and one-time spouse of Martin Scorsese (they made it one year). Life is a bear - a full-contact sport for sure - tough by design. If you disagree, you're probably not trying hard enough. Self-actualization is the understanding and acceptance of our flaws and defects, strengths and gifts, and putting them all to use in a satisfying way that benefits the greater good.

We lost a truly great one last month. Pulitzer Prize winning columnist, Charles Krauthammer, was a once in a generation human being. Known for his imposing and superhuman intellect and insight, he was celebrated for his humility, wonderful sense of humor, and genuine, genuine-ness. My mother-in-law gave me his book, "Things That Matter", about a month before he passed, and I've been savoring it ever since. It's a collection of his essays over the past thirty years on pretty much everything and should be required reading for pretty much everyone looking for some instructions on how to live a meaningful life. Krauthammer died of cancer. He was 68. In a final column published just weeks before he passed, he wrote, "I leave this life with no regrets. It was a wonderful life — full and complete with the great loves and great endeavors that make it worth living. I am sad to leave, but I leave with the knowledge that I lived the life that I intended." May we all be able to say the same.

August 2018

*"You can't go back and change the beginning, but you can
start where you are and change the ending."*

C. S. Lewis

I don't know about you, but I wouldn't go back if I could.
At 54, here are my thoughts on life by the decade. In our
20's, we don't know enough to be worried; 30's: Will things
ever work out; 40's: I sure hope things eventually work out;
50's: I think things just might work out; 60's: I can't believe
it's all worked out; 70's: I sure hope my grandkids can work
things out; 80's: What was I ever worried about?!

For a short period of time, we had both boys back under
the roof. Alex and Claire were here for a couple of weeks,
Collin about 5 days. Don't tell them I said so but it was nice.
Collin turned 21 since his last visit so we got to buy him his
first beer. The lad has turned "Greyhound-ing" into a verb as
his less-than-trusty Swag Wagon ™ can no longer be relied
on for any trips outside of Mickey's hometown. He jokingly
thanks sweet baby Jesus every time he steps through the dirty
bus doors at his destination and did so for the second to last
time in Fort Walton Beach. He'll begin his last semester later
this month and graduate to a career that hopefully leads

to Soundside Wealth Advisors sometime down the road. If that doesn't work, there could be an auto mechanic in the family. A trouble-shooting session with uncle John led to an internet search and YouTube video that pretty accurately described both the problem and potential fix for the old Saturn. RockAuto.com brought a new a new coil pack magically to his door in a few days and some borrowed tools brought an end to a pesky problem. Our newly minted 21-year-old, who'd just had his first beer, walked with a newfound swagger, sense of confidence and manliness that comes from facing down the man-versus-machine conflict, and kicking its ass. In my son's words, "Now all I need to do is buy a few motorcycles and I will be even closer to being Jon Kagan!" Obviously, I am very proud.

Pensacola has a special tradition on the second weekend of July. It's the homecoming show of the U.S. Navy flight demonstration team, the Blue Angels. It's a treat no matter how many times you've seen them. Flown over the waters of Pensacola Beach, this show is extra cool. We were one of hundreds (thousands?) of boats anchored off the beach. Prime seats and the water, even at 83 degrees, was a respite from the blistering heat of the afternoon. As usual, scores of extended-families travelled in for the weekend. We were quite a flotilla. Max, one of our grand-nephews from Orlando, went all European on us. But instead of topless, he shed his trunks and let it all air out. He's only 2 so I guess it's okay but when someone mentioned how nice it would be to be able to do the same, I thought, no thanks. Sunburn, chafing, and even with the water so warm, there's gonna be some shrinkage. Not to mention the possibility of a snagging and potential de-jones-ing injury. I'll take my board shorts thank you.

I had to channel my inner son-of-a-bitch last week, not a real big stretch, but one of those, "it's gonna hurt me more than you" moments. Our eldest son texted me a request. He wondered if I could see it in my heart to give him some cash for his trip to NYC before he starts his new career and collects his first paycheck. I'd been waiting for it since the lad had been living the life of leisure since graduation in May. Of course, I was going to help but there was no way I was going to reward his three-month vacation, so with buy-in from mom, I presented my plan. I would gladly "lend" him the cash if he worked up a 12-month repayment schedule which included a 5% surcharge. I had a similar arrangement with my dad about 30 years earlier, although I tacked on 10% - it was the 80's. Lesson learned.

I pen this monthly missive from my new digs. Alex and Claire left on a Monday morning and by Wednesday, my new home office was coming together nicely in what was Alex's bedroom. As they say on HGTV, it's a wonderful "space" - I should have kicked him out a long time ago. Funny thing. I saw one of Alex's old high school buddy's mom while roaming the aisles of Walmart for office supplies. After sharing my happy story, she told me about her husband's new model train room...where do you suppose he put it? I think things just might work out.

September 2018

"I am looking for a lot of men who have an infinite capacity to not know what can't be done"

Henry Ford

Double negatives aside, what a worthy quest. I guess you'd call that quality, drive. Kind of "punny", considering the quote-smith. Software developer Bud Tribble, in describing Steve Jobs' ability to get those around him to accomplish the seemingly impossible, used the term "reality distortion field", stolen from an old episode of Star Trek. Life's all about balance. Don't get me wrong, "smarts" is a good quality, but give me someone with a good dose of common-sense, grit, and drive and there's almost nothing we can't get done.

Labor Day has come and gone and with its passing, my white jeans have been locked away for the season. Thank goodness for my plaid corduroys. We've got a big Autumn in store. In just over 46 days, our son Alex will make an honest woman out of Claire Carpenter. She really doesn't need any help and I posit that she's getting the short end of the stick but details aside, we're very excited.

The couple has made their big move to Gotham City and have pretty much settled into their new digs. A few weeks back, they hopped on a plane in Denver with 5 loaded duffel bags representing all of their worldly possessions and arrived in the big apple after midnight. An Uber ride to the Air BnB and five flights of stairs later, they collapsed into their new temporary basecamp. Alex had been set up with a real estate agent, vetted by his new employer, and after a good night's rest, they got busy hunting some permanent digs. You might've heard that real estate in NYC can be a bit pricey. It also moves at lightning speed. The two had been scouring the internet for months, getting a feel for flats they could afford so they had a good idea of where and what they'd like to call home. They also learned that pictures on the internet can be deceiving and what they saw up close and personal was a bit of a letdown until they walked into what would end up being "the one". Their little slice of paradise is a second story unit, just under 400 square feet, in the upper east side on 78th and York. A rarity for a pad that size, they have 3 windows and an abundance of natural light, new appliances, and a clean bathroom. And perched above a Chinese restaurant, they've got built-in dinner for those nights they're too tired to throw some chicken on the George Foreman grill.

So I don't get accused of playing favorites, Collin had a busy month as well. I was hoping the lad would come home for a couple weeks and spend some time with me at the office. He's a finance major and will be graduating a semester early, just a couple months after his brother gets hitched. I wanted to get him excited about what a future career could look like. Alas, it wasn't meant to be. Turned out, he became a victim of his own success. As you know, he's been working as a Leasing Ambassador at the apartment complex where he resides. Apparently, his problem-solving and customer relations skills have been noticed by the higher ups. He was called into the big boss's office a few weeks back and as his father's son, expected the worst. He walked out with a new job, Sales Manager, which included a sporty raise. All those beatings seem to have paid off.

October 2018

> *"How often a man has cause to return thanks for the enthusiasms of his friends! They are the little fountains that run down from the hills to refresh the mental desert of the despondent."*
>
> Henry Van Dyke

Dilly dilly, Mr. Van Dyke. Life can be a bear. And for those who are lucky enough to have found their calling, many times the satisfaction comes from knowing that you're doing something that others are either unwilling or unable to do on their own. Deep Sea welding, Smoke-Jumping, Financial Planning ;-) The satisfaction comes from the challenge, outcomes, and differences made in the lives of real people. Thank the Lord for family and friends…friends in particular, since family is expected to be there.

Collin got a big promotion and with it, his first corporate retreat. The company flew him up to Atlanta for a two-day indoc and company update. The kid was beside himself with excitement, "Dad, they're paying for my airplane ticket, hotel room and everything!" My only advice was not to do anything stupid or use alcohol as an anxiolytic. It was an excellent experience for the lad and the first time in his young professional life that he was treated like an adult. After the first day's sessions, he found himself having cocktails with the CFO and CIO. Since he's still employed, I guess it went okay. Of course, we're excited for him but at the same time, I suggested he keep his options open for other post-graduation opportunities, particularly in the area of finance since there just might be a place for him in a Wealth Advisory group I'm pretty familiar with. Just when I'd thought I might have lost him to the real estate sector, the week he returned to his new job, he was tasked with tending to a potential rumble between a group of tenants. On the way to the scene, he was informed that one of the tenants had a firearm. I think I've still got a shot.

November 2018

The skies poured fury as I set out west, on motorbike. Destination...Seville Square in downtown Pensacola. The giant oak trees would provide little shelter to the 200 or so gathered to witness the marriage of Alex and Claire. Thanks goodness Claire opted for a tent a few days prior. Celebrants had come from far and wide, spanning both coasts and of course Tuscaloosa (Roll Tide). The rain did little to dampen the mood. Truthfully, it added a serene, New Orleans bayou vibe under the canopy of the mighty two-hundred plus year old sentries of the square. Alex, as you might expect from years of these missives, remained cool, calm, and totally unshaken. He was Alex. Pastor Scott and the parents of the bride, Daniel and Cynthia, the same. The Heavenly Spirit was in the house. It didn't hurt that the bar was opened early as we waited for what brother-in-law Boo, a professional pilot, reported as the last band of the storm to pass. On cue, the rain stopped and we got down to business.

Vows complete, food in our bellies, we put on our boogie shoes and got down. Claire hired a rocking band from Mobile and I'd imagine we entertained them nearly as much as they entertained us. In my 55 orbits of the sun, I've been a best-man, groom, and father-of the groom. Arguably, the most stressful role is that of best man. The toast. Collin did not disappoint. His "Jewish entertainment gene" kicked into overdrive and he delivered, big. When all was said it done, the gig went down exactly as we'd hoped, as Alex and Claire got on my big, shiny (wet), red motorcycle and rode through the crowd and into the rest of their lives. Huge shout to our HBIC (Head Bitch in Charge), Carrie. We had no shortage of both Indians and Chiefs and Carrie skillfully utilized all in order to bring all the parts of this machine together. We love you Mama Begs.

Rewind a couple afternoons prior. The boys came into town on Thursday and that afternoon, the three of us hung out on the deck, enjoying a cold one and shooting the breeze. Collin shared the duties of his new job and his role in managing and motivating seven direct reports. I waited for Alex to fill his usual role of big brother, one upping with grand tales of his new pursuit in Manhattan. Instead, he answered with praise, support, and encouragement, working to get his younger sibling duly pumped up for his upcoming job fairs. For those out there with kids still onboard, hang in there. It is truly a beautiful thing to witness your offspring make the transition from dependent to independent. To be able to put down your guard and take in your kids as fellow adults is a one of the greatest joys in the universe. Probably a pretty cool thing from the other side as well.

December 2018

"When you get hit in the face 5, 6, 7 times, you start catching."

Terry Griffin

S aid the father of one-handed NFL star, Shaquem Griffin, when asked how he taught his son to catch a football. Shaqhem and his identical-twin brother Shaquill, former stars at the University of Central Florida, now suit up for the Seattle Seahawks. A painful birth defect led to the amputation of the younger brother's left hand at four years old. His parents decided against a prosthetic. Mom, Tangie, said he didn't need it. He taught himself to button his shirt, tie his shoes, anything he needed to do, he did. When asked how he'd finally know he'd been successful, the inspirational young man answered, "When it's not about me being one-handed, it's about me being a great player." No hyphens, no labels, no limits, no excuses. Great lesson for us all.

Collin has long cried foul over our obvious display of favoritism. We'd joined Alex for a half dozen Alabama football games but in his four-year stint in Orlando, we'd never done the same with our #2 son. We assured him it was all about the seven-hour drive (and the fact that we loved

Alex more) but that, surprisingly, did little to comfort the lad. So, it was that we found ourselves in the land of the Knights to catch our first and last UCF football game before Collin joins the ranks of alumnus. It was also my first visit to the kid's apartment. Lovely from the outside, we stepped through the front door and were immediately smacked in the face by the swirling aroma of spilt beer, spoiled milk, and feet. On the spot I made the decision to never, ever own a rental property in a college town. Kickoff was 8:00 pm so we had the day to play around town and explore the sprawling campus of Florida's fastest growing university. The contrast with Alabama was striking. Both are beautiful and obviously very well capitalized. UCF is significantly more laid back. Nowhere was this more evident than the pregame tailgate party. Alabama's pregame party at the quad is legendary. A wall-to-wall celebration across the expansive turf, filled with equal part sharp-dressed students and dedicated alumnus, dressed out in khaki's, crimson and pretty party dresses. Flash to Florida and this madhouse was mostly a student affair, geezers like us were in the minority. There was a lot of skin, tights, and tats (tattoos, get your head out of the gutter, people!) The big screen TVs in the tents at Alabama were replaced with beer pong and beer bongs. I've got to say that we had a lot of fun playing college 2.0 with Collin's friends. I think I lost 30 years that afternoon. And what a game! The Knight's football team is on a nearly 2-year win streak. Usually under-appreciated for an arguably light schedule, this game against 9-1 Cincinnati was host to ESPN's College Game Day and we were buckled in for a good show. We were not disappointed. Cincinnati was physically huge. I would not want to have to plan the Thanksgiving meal for those boys. They grabbed the early momentum with a sack of UCF quarterback McKenzie Milton in the end zone. Six nothing. But then it got fun. UCF was surgical. Their defense completely shut down Cincinnati's passing game. On offense, Hawaiian born quarterback, McKenzie Milton had a brilliant arm and connected all night with his deft receivers. When all was done, it was 38-13, UCF.

UCF dayz

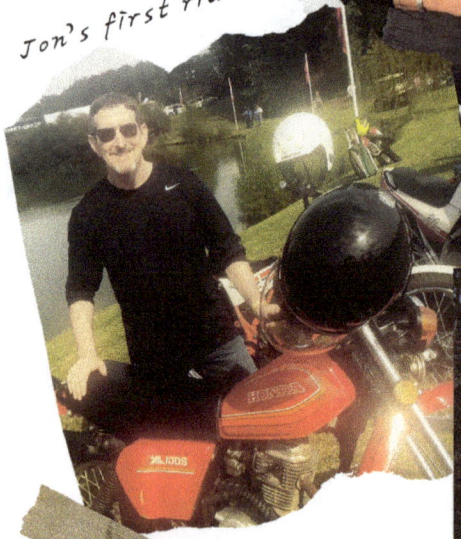
Jon's first ride

No guts no glory

UPPER TATTLETALE

EXPERT ONLY

kagan cousins

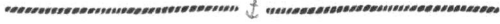

2019

January 2019

"There is no definition of a successful life that does not include service to others."

George H. W. Bush

The only modern U.S. President to NOT write a memoir, when 41 passed, we heard many a story of what defines a truly good human being. Ron Rowe, U.S. Secret Service Deputy Assistant Director, shared the time in 2013, when Timberwolf (GHWB's callsign) learned that the two-year old son of one of his Secret Service agents was battling leukemia. Childhood leukemia had touched the Bush's in the past. Their three-year old granddaughter, Robin, lost her battle in 1953. Without a second thought, the President joined the rest of the security detail and shaved his head bald in solidarity with the boy's fight. Quite a Google-worthy picture and just one example of a life well-lived.

Christmas was crazy this year. It's always about the kids, and the young-ins' were plentiful. First get together was at Annie's house. There is no argument, she is the best mother-in-law in the universe. And she can throw a party. The customary meal is meatball grinders (I think she lived in New Jersey once), and afterwards we all exchange mostly gag gifts. This year, she added a new event. We all know that Annie's got connections but we were shocked to learn she's got an in with St. Nick himself. She had a pile of letters from Santa Claus addressed to all of her great grand nieces and nephews at the party. These letters were read to said young-in by the respective parent. Third up was a letter to Ellie, the 18-month-old daughter of Sarah whom I wrote about last year. Sarah is a single-mom. Ellie's father has no involvement, by design. Though the situation is not traditional, there is not a sweeter, more loved little girl anywhere. That said, Sarah has been dating Derek for about 9 months. This guy is the salt of the Earth. A country boy from Jay, FL, combat Air Force veteran, and father of two daughters of his own from a previous marriage. We all had fingers crossed that this would turn into something more. Well, here's Ellie's letter from Santa, "Since I met you at one, I've watched you grow...Now we're celebrating our first Christmas together, ho, ho, ho! I'm sure you've asked Santa for so many things, as we all listen to the jingle bells ring...But one thing I want you to have, is someone that one day you can call dad. So, ask your mom now, but ask her with ease...Mom I kind of like Dee-Dee, will you marry him please?" There was not a dry eye in the house (dang, I'm crying again!)

Kathleen is the baby in her family. It's been our Christmas Eve tradition to have Annie spend the night, so she can get up with our kids (her youngest grandchildren) and watch them open presents. We always watch a movie, and it's not always seasonal. More often than not, it's a real stinker... usually selected by me (I can't be good at everything ;) . This year, Collin got the honors and as we scanned the selections on Amazon Prime, he came across one that a friend from school told him was solid. All I can say is, like father, like son. "The Florida Project" started out bad, and got worse. Nothing says Christmas like a movie about a profane, tattoo-covered prostitute living in a cheap motel in the hoods of south Florida, from the eyes of her funny, cynical, street-smart, little daughter. Puts a new twist in Ho, Ho, Ho! Thanks Collin, for taking the heat off of me. Collin Facetimed his friend right after the movie who defended his reputation saying, "I didn't say it was a Christmas movie!"

March 2019

What are you afraid of? Failure. Pain. Disappointment. Spiders. Other than those six-legged, miniature beasts from hell, the rest all focus on what could go wrong. What if instead, we shifted our thoughts to what could go right? Unhappy with your current career? Do some thoughtful planning, get some help if needed, and execute. Current relationship going nowhere? (not you, Kathleen ;-)) Ditto. Picked up an extra 30 pounds over the years? Same. The truth is, we are often our own worst enemies. The reason we are not achieving all that we could is because we listen to those voices in our head that inject doubt and fear. Maybe it's time for some new voices.

__Swag__ / adjective / derivative of swag·ger / 1. Marked by elegance or showiness: POSH. Wagon / noun / wag·on / 1. a four-wheeled vehicle for transporting bulky commodities and drawn originally by animals: CART. Collin picked up his trusty chariot as a High School Junior. Nicknamed the Swag-Wagon, his 2004 Saturn LW 300 station wagon served him faithfully over the years. It provided freedom in High

School, countless round-trips to school in Orlando, and very likely, shelter during an East Coast surfing trip or two. But it was tired, and just as a cowboy eventually retires his trusty steed, the lad preparing to graduate, had to look the future. Enter Old Blue. A shiny, new-to-him, 2008 Toyota Four Runner. With just over 170,000 miles on the clock, this filly is barely broken-in. Collin is looking forward to a future filled with many adventures on his new mount and we are excited for him.

The biggest question for #2 son is who's going to be signing his paycheck in a few months? May 3rd is graduation day and although he's currently gainfully employed, word is he's looking to break into the world of finance. Collin's a great kid, we get along reasonably well, and my practice has grown to the point where I could keep another planner occupied. You know where this is going. I let the idea percolate for a number of weeks before putting fingers to keyboard and tapping out a real job offer. It's good, not great. Frankly, he'd earn more by starting at a big national firm and, stepping back, I really hope he goes that route. Selfishly though, I think I'd enjoy having him around. The risk is that we're so similar that after a month or two, we'd have a blowup that leads to fifteen or so years of no communication…not unheard of in Kagan-lore. As the President says, "We'll see what happens."

At one point during my time as Navy helicopter pilot, I was a Detachment Maintenance Officer. I was responsible for keeping our trusty SH-2F "Sea Sprite" flying and had about 14 outstanding maintainers of all stripes under my wing who turned the wrenches, banged the hammers, and worked the test equipment needed to keep *Easyrider 58* in the air. When the work was complete, it was my job as check pilot, to certify the aircraft mission capable. I loved that job and currently get the same satisfaction with motorbikes, a story for a different time. To keep us safe and efficient, one of the many programs in place was Tool Control. It's been said that Helicopters are a collection of thousands of parts, spinning at high rates of speed, all trying to get away from each other. You can imagine an errant tool, left in the wrong place, could cause some death and destruction. Enter the Tool Control program.

Fast forward about 28 years. My wife is the Maintenance Officer of our household. Since I'd rather be on two wheels in my off-time, it's usually Kathleen who lets me know when things need to be repaired, replaced, or just banged on with a big hammer. Enter, *Pad Control*. Kathleen is a kick-ass manager. After folding a freshly laundered load of clothes, she realized a pad was missing from one of her female under-garments (she's gonna kill me!) When it failed to turn up after a few more days, she got on google to investigate the potential hiding places. She landed on the possibility of it sneaking into the washing machine's water pump assembly. Wouldn't you know, a few days later, our 15-year-old washing machine stopped in mid-cycle, failing to drain. This happened about 6 months ago and at that time, Dr. Google helped me diagnose and change a faulty lid switch. This time, it directed me to the water pump assembly and after about 45 minutes of bailing water, wrenching and banging, I had the pump in my hand and pulled out the culprit. Mystery solved. Thanks once again to *Google* and *YouTube*. I'm thinking of starting a home-based surgery practice next. Give us a call to get on the calendar.

April 2019

Words can be tricky things. We were honored to host a rehearsal dinner for nephew Jack Begley and his beautiful fiancé Kerrie Shaw. It was the second such event in the past year and we've got one more coming up this fall. The weather was perfect and everything went exactly as we'd all hoped. I've known Jack since he was about four. I've known his friends for about 15 years so it was great to catch up with everyone on such a happy occasion. I particularly enjoyed talking with Cody, Jack's long-time soccer buddy, now a Navy jet pilot in training in Kingsville, TX. It was so fun to relive those flight school memories and visit with such a fine young man. But after a pretty young woman joined the conversation, I felt like I was at best monopolizing his time, at worst, cramping his style. I said, "I'm going to leave you to talk with more interesting people" and took my leave. Of course, what I meant was, "I'm going to leave, so you can talk with more interesting people" but as I walked away, I thought they probably heard, "I'm going to leave you, so I can talk with more interesting people." By that time, it was too late to go back and explain, like trying to explain a joke that didn't work. I guess I've transitioned from Jack's creepy uncle to Jack's creepy and rude uncle.

No more barriers to entry. The wedding weekend was a blast. Our boys made it home for the event but the visit was fleeting. Alex hit the road early Sunday morning. It's tax season and the kid is slammed. Collin and I did the same, both off to Orlando, me for a financial conference, Collin for life in general. I decided to head out a day early and go visit my folks in Sarasota for a quick visit. My pop just turned 85 and though we've gone through some storms over the years, we're at a really good place right now. In fact, it was the best visit I've ever had with the old man. Most of us put up walls to keep others from seeing our vulnerabilities. It's a wonderful thing when those walls come down. In 30 years or so, my own kids might see that I'm not as big an ogre as they thought. As for the financial conference, Collin came down for a solid day and I've got to say, I enjoyed the hell out of that kid. I even took the lead from my dad, and dropped my guard. I hugged him and got all misty when he left, letting him know how proud I am of whom he's become and how much I love him. Hope I'm not getting soft.

Got a light? I hope I don't hurt any feelings but I'm going to say it. Of all the extended family, *the Juder* takes the highest spot on the podium. A woman of exceptional character and equal quirks, you can read about her in her son's book, "Un Moving Four Ward" http://www.bobbellbooks.com/ My champion's single vice has always been nicotine. The Juder can do some damage to a pack of smokes. At 81, it's caught up to her, hospice is involved, but Judy is facing the inevitable as she's faced all of the challenges she's conquered along her fantastic voyage. With faith, humor, and *lady-balls*. Kathleen and I stopped by for a visit and caught her asleep after a long day. We left, grabbed a bite to eat, and ended up stopping by afterwards with a bag of leftovers. We arrived at the Pensacola home where Judy raised two kids and has lived for nearly 50 years, greeted by her daughter Karen. Did I tell you Judy was a smoker? We all took a seat in the living room and as Judy lit up, I said, "Give me one of those." Now it's been a long time since I smoked anything and the last time, it probably wasn't tobacco. That said, it was an honor having a smoke with my hero and friend. We also split a PBR. God, I love this family.

May 2019

There is no substitute for experience. It can't be bought. It can't be taught. It can't be inherited. It has to be lived. I remember a time, decades back, when I literally thought to myself, "I've had a great run. I've seen so much, lived so much, experienced so much. If my time was up today, I'm okay with that." I was 21. How funny to look back and realize how little I knew. How little I'd seen. How little I'd experienced. I imagine that 20 years from now, I'll think back to penning this piece and realize the same.

Lessons from the Madness. March Moto Madness celebrates the end of moto-hibernation with camping, riding, and general fellowship, with similarly afflicted practitioners. The original "Mother Rally", held in Tellico Plains, TN, dates back to 2006 and is now joined by dozens around the world. I loaded my truck with a street bike, a dirt bike, and camping gear to join over 800 folks from around the country for my second visit to this mecca of moto-exploring. The riding was epic. Off-road "single-track" trails twisting up, down, and around the Smoky Mountains, and legendary pavement like the Cherohala Skyway and Tail of the Dragon. Put away those images of Hell's Angels, chains and leather. The first day of riding began with a prayer. Ryan, our ride leader, was a long-time member of the Christian Motorcyclists Association, and his words set the tone perfectly as the nine of us set out on our trailbikes to explores God's beautiful creation. <u>Lesson one</u>: Everything is better if you begin with gratitude. About 5 miles in, Ryan had a minor spill that degraded the performance of his machine and as a result, I took the lead. <u>Lesson two</u>...always be prepared to serve. Minor mishap behind us, the remaining 80 miles were tremendous. Challenging terrain. Spectacular scenery. Great workout. With plenty of daylight left, I grabbed a quick bite and jumped on my street-bike for a few hours of heavenly asphalt. Made it home for barbecue, live music, and outstanding fellowship. The night was perfect sleeping bag weather and it was a duly-earned slumber. <u>Lesson 3</u>: Camping shows you just how little you really need.

After a good night's rest, hearty breakfast, and a marginal bowel movement, the highlight of day two was a riding class that I'll admit, had given me a bit of pause since enrolling online. Tom Asher is the stuff of legend. In 2016, his skills earned him a spot on Team U.S. to compete for the BMW GS Trophy in Thailand. Now, in addition to his day job, he holds clinics at these rally's, teaching us mortals how to ride our big, heavy, adventure motorcycles in places that few dare to tread. There was a beginner, Intermediate, and Advanced class and I planned on the intermediate option. Turns out the only available spot was at the grown-up table in the advanced class. No Guts, no Glory...I signed up. My only fear was I'd be THAT GUY...the one that held up the group and prevented us from doing everything on the syllabus. Like most of our anxieties, it was misplaced. What a class. We learned how to pilot our 500 lb. bikes down a steep embankment and cross a rocky stream, to climb steep mountain trails, to jump a fallen log across a trail when there is no way around it. He taught us to slow down, be deliberate with every movement, every line, always purposeful and in control. It was a transformational riding experience. Lesson's 4 & 5: Most of our fears are between our ears & sometimes, in order to grow, you should take the rocky path.

Later that afternoon, I decided to break camp as a nasty storm was forecast to arrive that evening and last through the next day. The load-up was uneventful, but as I turned out of the rally site onto the country road, I clipped a broken metal guardrail with my right rear truck tire, tearing it instantly. I pulled aside and as I surveyed the situation, a young man came by and told me what I'd done. As I instinctively went to full-blown self-degradation mode, my new friend advised I slow down, relax, and chill. "Don't be so hard on yourself. It'll be okay. Hell, I'm getting divorced." Perspective. I thanked him for the slap in the face, gave him my card and told him to call me Monday. I'm a financial planner and I've specialized in divorce for years. I told him I'd help him make smart decisions and wouldn't charge him a thing. Lesson 6: It's funny how God puts us exactly where we need to be.

June 2019

So answered the 96-year-old creator of Archie & Edith
Bunker, George & Louise Jefferson, and Fred & Lamont
Sanford, to the question, "What's the best and worst thing
about still working at age 96." What a wonderful approach to
life at any age.

Talk about Aiming High. A family emergency brought
my bull-riding barber back to Panama City so I'm back
at East Hill Barbershop… a hip joint, with a barber pole
out front and the sweet smell of antiseptic and aftershave
wafting in the air. I was a walk-in so I got the new guy. Rick,
a massive human being, fully bearded and tatted, was new
to the shop, but in the trade for a couple of decades. Like
the rest of the fellas, he's a big teddy bear. As Rick did what
he could to my cowlicked mane, a pretty female walked in
and took the on-deck chair by Rick. Dressed in a flight suit,
her squadron patch indicated Navy Primary Flight training.
For the un-initiated, budding Naval Aviators all begin with

primary. We learn how to put a high performance fixed-wing aircraft through its paces. Basic take off & landings and pattern work, instruments, formation, aerobatics, the whole deal. From there, depending on how we've done and more importantly, the needs of the Navy (Marine Corps and Coast Guard go through the same program), we move on or "select", to advanced training and one of three pipelines: jets, props, or helicopters. Us old has-beens never pass up the opportunity to relive the glory days with those in the early stages of theirs, so I asked her what she wanted to fly. "Space ships I hope" was her answer. How's that for ambition?

FREEEDOOOOOM! Graduation came to the Kagan household in a big way. After 23 years of raising kids, we're finally done (I think I just heard God laughing.) Our youngest graduated from the University of Central Florida (UCF) with a degree in finance. Better yet, Collin was offered and accepted a job in his chosen field. I told you last month that I'd made him an offer to come work with me. Not too surprisingly, he made me proud and turned me down. The lad was not ready to settle down to small-town living. He loved the hustle and bustle of Orlando and decided to give it a go in the big city. UCF has a great placement program and Collin got interviews with four firms. One stood out for him for their culture, history, and the great rapport he'd established with the complex manager. But they really made him work for it. After two interviews, the price of admission to number three was a test of his initiative and networking skills. He was tasked with sending questionnaires to folks in his universe. He needed at least fifty to take the time to complete them in order to get the next interview. Game over if it were it me at age 22. Not so for our #2 son. Not only did he get the 50 responses, one of them, a young man who used to work for Collin at the apartment complex, shot him a text. It turned out his uncle had just retired from the firm of interest and apparently was quite a big shot. He put Collin in touch with Uncle Big and the rest, as they say, was history.

You Can Go Home Again. After graduation, I had an ambitious goal. I hoped to pull off what would arguably be the biggest family reunion in Kagan history. Alex and Claire had flown down from New York. My parents live about two hours south of Orlando in Sarasota. I've written of my on-again, off-again relationship with my pop. I love and respect the guy beyond words and wouldn't be me without him. Like many fathers and sons, our relationship was complicated. I'll spare you the psychobabble but suffice it to say that a big casualty of that dysfunction was that our own kids did not get to know their grandfather and were missing an important link to who they are. The last time our eldest son Alex saw my pop, said son was a screaming, colicky, one-month old at Thanksgiving dinner. With all of us in such close proximity and our relationship at the best place it's ever been, I called my mom to craft a plan (for the record, Henry Kissinger wouldn't return my phone calls.) We decided on dinner at their favorite restaurant in town and a 5:15 pm rendezvous, midnight in Sarasota time. I will admit, I was scared sh#tless. Mentally, I'm already damaged goods but my kids have their whole lives in front of them and I sure didn't want to mess that up if things went sideways. We made the drive, arrived early, but it turned out there were two of these restaurants within five miles of each other, both equidistant from my folk's house. I made my choice and upon arrival, I left the gang in the car to check the restaurant. It turned out my folks were doing the same. When we saw each other, my dad broke out in the biggest smile I'd ever seen on that mug of his... I'm misty as I type. We had a wonderful time. My kids learned a lot about their roots in that restaurant and my dad got to see that his #1 son did okay. With any luck, we'll do it again in a different venue. If you've got a similar history with someone important to you, consider making an effort at reconciliation. Just think what could happen if things go right.

August 2019

> "Be humble. Be hungry. And always be the hardest worker in the room."
>
> Dwayne "the Rock" Johnson

Work. There is no substitute. Luck is nice, but you've probably heard the old saying, "the harder I work, the luckier I get." There's nothing wrong with being born-well... the "lucky sperm club" as they say. That said, the history is full of privileged offspring who never reach escape velocity. "The Rock" hit the nail on the head with his answer to the question, "What is the key to success?"

Everyone knows the two best days in the life of a boat owner are the day you buy it and the day you sell it. At a recent Rotary lunch, our guest speaker gave a twist to that old saw. According to our guest, the answer to the Jeopardy question, "The two best days in the life of a parent" is "What is the day you bring little junior home and the day he's finally off your payroll?" I sure hope that's not the case because I just signed not-so-little junior's first paycheck with Soundside Wealth Advisors.

In May, I wrote that our son Collin, with a freshly printed Bachelor of Science degree in Finance in hand, turned down the offer to join his old man's practice. I was a bit sad, a bit relieved (yah, I was a little scared of the big change), but proud of the kid's decision to give it a go in Orlando. He'd set down some roots over the past four years and was comfortable in his routine and social network. He accepted an offer with an old-line, respected firm and got busy. Alas, the weeks went by, and when junior would awaken in the middle of the night, his mind was uneasy. Was he on the right track? We spoke often, he's my kid after all and I kind of like him most of the time. I did not, and would not ever to tell him what to do. I did a lot of listening and questioning and in the end, suggested he talk with his "Uncle" Jorge. I've written many times of Jorge and Gina, our neighbors of close to 15 years, who never had kids of their own, but who's wisdom make them a sought-out source of feedback for folks of all ages. As is often the case, Gina is sweet, sensitive, funny, beautiful on the inside and out, while Jorge is… Jorge. He will not hesitate to give you his opinion…directly. As I've aged, I've actually tried to channel my inner Jorge when approaching a problem…WWJD? He has a unique ability to distill an issue to its core components and make unemotional decisions that just tend to make sense. Collin spoke with Jorge and a couple days later, so did I. When Collin and I next spoke, he said he'd reconsidered my offer, and would like to accept. I couldn't be more excited and, funny thing, after speaking with Jorge, I'm no longer scared (well, maybe a little). Stand by for progress reports.

Alex is approaching his one-year anniversary with the accounting firm. Career aside, he and Claire have been busy as you'd expect of any young couple living smack dab in the middle of New York City. They've recently expanded their horizons literally, moving from an apartment the size of a large closet to one the size of a large bedroom. Not quite the Jefferson's, but pretty cool none-the-less. Career-wise, Alex told us he was called by a head-hunter. I was shocked. The kid's got less than a year on the job… as dashing, intelligent, and all-in-all wonderful as he is, what could he possibly bring to the table? Apparently, that's a pretty common part of life in the big city, especially for folks in a big four accounting firm. Alex took the call…why not? He's not leaving his firm but he did learn a little more about what he's worth in the marketplace. And he's doing great there. His supervisor gave him the nickname, AK-47. AK are his initials, but he when he glanced back quizzically, said supervisor said, "Left un-supervised, you do some real damage." That's my boy!

September 2019

Mr. Trejo is a likely winner of the contest for the man you'd least want to meet in a dark alley. As a youth, he was an over-achiever when it came to hell-raising. His resume includes stints at Folsom and San Quentin prisons. In 1968, while serving time at the latter, he was facing a possible death sentence for his role in a prison riot. "We went to the hole and were facing the gas chamber," Trejo solemnly recounted to Ryan Parker of the Hollywood Reporter. "And I remember asking God, 'Let me die with dignity. Just let me say goodbye. And if you do, I will say your name every day, and I will do whatever I can for my fellow man." God came through and so did Mr. Trejo, big time. For a powerful story of redemption, Google his name.

"How do you get to Carnegie Hall?" "Practice, practice, practice." So how do you become a financial planner? Collin will tell you…Study, study, study. The kid's been hitting the books, hard. He's three exams in with one more to go before I cut the ribbon and make it official. Last week was the big one. The Securities and Exchange Commission (SEC) Series 7 General Securities exam. When I entered the industry 20 years ago, the firm I was attached to had a policy. You get one shot…pass the test or pack your bags. It made sense, as a business, they made choices on deploying their resources. A business owner myself, now I make the calls. I let my son know that I believe in him, BUT, if he downed that test, he'd find work elsewhere, take a year to "mature", then reapply if he chose to do so. So, at the testing center, when the lad hit "submit" for the last time, there was an agonizing instant before the computer screen announced his fate. PASS. I don't know who was more relieved.

Kathleen has been a runner since, forever. Several months back, she was invited to join the "My Pink Lawyer" running team, captained by our friend and estate planning attorney, Kristen Marks. Now Kristen is not your run-of-the-mill enthusiast. She's a member of that crazy cohort for whom 26.2 miles is not enough. She's an Ultra Marathoner and recently completed the famed Antelope Canyon Ultra in the Arizona desert. Kathleen had a couple ½ marathons under her belt but had always wondered if she could pull off the Full Monty. For a runner, to be able to put that 26.2 sticker on the back of your car is a coveted accomplishment. Well, last month, not only did Kathleen make it happen, I joined her. Before you think too highly of our achievement, you've got to take a closer look at the sticker. We ran our first Leprechaun Marathon…26.2…feet. Okay so it wasn't much of a run, but it was really hot that afternoon. Thanks Kristen and company for the honor of representing your team at the 2nd Annual O'Reilly's Uptown Pub event in Pensacola. See you next year.

October 2019

I miss the days when you could tune into the Tonight Show to decompress before turning in. You could always count on Johnny Carson and his successor, Jay Leno, to be funny and keep politics out of their shtick. In fact, you never really knew what side of the aisle they sat. Johnny Carson once said, "I got hate-mail from both sides!" The September 21st edition of the Wall Street Journal had a great story on Leno in its Gears & Gadgets column. On relaxing, Leno shares, "It's not that I can't. I don't want to. I'll relax when I have my stroke. I've got a pool that I've never been in. Well, I went in 28 years ago to fix the light." Now that's funny.

The year was 1995. I was 9 years into the Navy, 2 years into my marriage. Flying helicopters was a kick. Throw in the travel and you've got an unbeatable lifestyle for a young single man. Add a wife and new son and it's a whole new ballgame. I was at what a pilot calls a "go/no-go" point and I chose go. Next came the scary part...job search. A Marine Corps friend had done the same a year earlier and landed a job in pharmaceutical sales. After conferring with my old pal, I was all-in. I worked several angles and managed to score an interview with a regional manager for major player in the industry. In the interview, I let it be known that I'd go anywhere for the opportunity to work for this firm. Be careful what you wish for. We soon found ourselves headed north to western Kentucky. Kind of like the Beverly Hillbillies in reverse. My toughest sales pitch was convincing Kathleen to stay with me long enough to get us back to Florida. As you know, it all worked out, and last month, I made my first return visit to the birth state of Abraham Lincoln and our son Collin. Had a great time at the Land between the Lakes Dual Sport motorcycle event outside of Cadiz, KY. No injuries or break downs and great weather for camping made for an excellent outing. Kathleen stayed home. In the case of the Bluegrass state, absence did not make the heart grow fonder. Okay, maybe it was the camping ;)

Our niece Sarah found that sometimes, the best way to get ahead is to marry one. We were honored to host Mr. & Mrs. Derek Head's wedding reception in our backyard last month. Believe it or not, the couple initially met through Facebook. Seeing they had a mutual friend (Sarah's step-brother, Wesley) he took the site's suggestion to send our pretty niece a friend request. Was it love at first click? Not quite. Sarah's not just a pretty face. She did her research before accepting. Clicked on his profile, she couldn't help but notice picture after picture of his two beautiful daughters, Gracie (7) and Nora (2 ½). Upon further investigation, she learned that he was a solid, principled, hard-working, family-man, a USAF veteran crew chief, currently serving in the reserves. Due diligence complete, next came the scary part…sending a message. I always say, "no guts, no glory" and Sarah, never short on guts, hit "send". One week, hours of Facetime, talking on the phone, and countless texts later, Derek was on the road from his digs in Thomasville, Georgia for their first date. You could say it went pretty well. Exactly six months later, he popped the question at a family event that I wrote about at the time. As Sarah said, "Derek fit right into our family like the missing piece I never thought I'd find. He's simply my person." We couldn't agree more and are absolutely thrilled to have him join the chaos. As an added bonus to an already blessed occasion, our very own newlyweds made the trip from New York city to share in the festivities. Alex and Claire are doing great. Working hard, playing occasionally, and taking in all that life in "the city that never sleeps has to offer". As for them, they slept in each day till after 10:00 so I guess they were catching up on some lost zzzzz's. No judgement, it was wonderful to see them. They stayed for just under a week. Claire just landed a new job that hadn't yet started and Alex was able to work remotely so he burned almost no vacation time. Great stuff.

If you are really, really observant, you might have noticed another Kagan in the footer of this letterhead. It's official, Collin is a financial advisor. He passed his 4th and final exam and is now a fully-licensed part of the team. Sandy and I couldn't be more excited (Collin's pretty tickled himself). He's already fit in like one of the better fingers of a glove. It is true. There is no substitute for experience. After 20 years and two once-in-a-lifetime market corrections, there's not a lot that surprises me. That said, technology is changing so quickly these days and the lubrication between my neural synapses is not as fresh as it used to be. There's a lot to be said for new blood and millennials who've grown up in the digital-age. Collin will be both my Chief Technology Officer and Chief Marketing Officer. I've always said that I am never retiring and bringing my son onboard has made me even less likely to fade into the sunset. I'm more energized than ever and have shifted into growth mode now that I have an extra teammate and added capacity. For those interested, we're working on a series of educational webinars where you'll be able to participate from the comfort of your lazy boy and fuzzy pants. Stay tuned.

November 2019

I'd wager that this statement was so remarkably received because most of us can't imagine making it under similar circumstances. The young man had recently lost his older brother at the hands of the woman he'd addressed. It was a tragic mistake that took his life, and changed hers forever. At her sentencing, she apologized to the family, asked for God's forgiveness, and stated that she hates herself every single day for what she'd done. Then came Brandt's statement and the hug seen round the world. Could I have done the same? I don't know and hopefully, will never find out. But I know one thing for sure. The world needs more Brandt Jeans.

We'd survived a wedding reception in our back yard. The weather held out, there were no stabbings or law enforcement involvement of any kind. We decided to treat ourselves to a north Georgia getaway for some relaxation and a little leaf-peeping. A friend told us about the "Misty

Mountain Inn and Cabins" in Blairsville. Fans of Hobbits and Led Zeppelin, how could we say no. I led the way on the motorcycle, Kathleen followed in the truck, and ten hours later we pulled into the gravel driveway of the Serenity cabin. Beautiful country. Blairsville is a quaint little mountain town in northwest Georgia, about 2 hours past Atlanta in the shadow of Brasstown Bald, Georgia's highest peak. It's the land of waterfalls, the beginning of the Appalachian Trail, and a wonderful place to escape the daily grind. That was until Kathleen woke up with some awful pain in her lower right abdominal quadrant. We'd planned a day trip to Highlands, Georgia with a nice motorcycle ride, mountain hike, and dinner at a hip restaurant recommended by a friend. It quickly became apparent that Kathleen was dealing with more than just indigestion. She was hurting, but mobile, so we decided to pack up, load the motorcycle into the truck, and head home. Ten hours later, we pulled into our driveway and called it an early night.

Guys, we may think we're tough, but when it comes to pain tolerance, women put us to shame. Kathleen woke up the following morning, glad to be home and feeling a little better. It wasn't until 3 days later when back at work, her partner in crime hit her with the ultrasound. The attending physician who just happened to be a gastroenterologist took a look and strongly suggested further diagnostics. A CT scan the following morning confirmed the diagnosis, the offending gland was getting evicted. Three hours later, she was in recovery, minus one badly inflamed appendix. We went home that night and a few days later, all was right again in Mudville.

Non-medically, we had a nice development. Collin is on his own. Having passed all his licensing exams, the lad moved from training-pay to a position where, with some careful planning, he just might be able to support himself. After a fairly exhaustive search, my new junior partner secured himself a very cool bachelor pad in downtown Pensacola's North Hill district. For those outside of the area, Pensacola's downtown scene has completely metamorphosized over the past 10 years. It is a truly hip place with so much going on, particularly for the younger crowd. Collin is right in the thick of it all and on the weekend, a bicycle will get him anywhere he needs to go. He's in an older, two-story brick quadplex, with lots of windows and a covered porch area where he can hang out, sip Mojitos and read Hemingway (he won't, but he could ;)

December 2019

I'm reading the general's memoir, "Call Sign Chaos... Learning to Lead." Wow. Nickname, Mad Dog, is a misnomer. The General's tenacity and charisma are matched equally by his wits and brain-power. This is one of the best books on leadership I've ever read. As the paragraphs fell, his words actually induced adrenalin. He takes the reader through his life in the Corps; his entry was one of those jail or service deals, but once inside, the service sculpted him into a leader of leaders. You may have heard that life comes with no instructions. Wrong. You just need to know where to look.

The Turkey Trot is an annual gathering of off-road moto-enthusiasts of all ages who come from all over the southeast to romp through the long leaf pine forest and deep white sand of the FL panhandle. In its 11th year, basecamp was once again the Blackwater State Forest, Wilderness Landing campground, about 12 miles east of the tiny town of Baker. It's primitive camping - no electricity or water hookup but there is a nice restroom and access to the iconic Blackwater River. It's hosted by the Pensacola Area Riders and organized this year by yours truly since our illustrious leader of the past, retired to the mountains of TN. Riding the trails of Blackwater is my therapy. It's a beautiful and spiritual place, I call it the Church of the Woods and I spend many a Sabbath there. Riding in the forest is like motorized-hiking. You share all the sights, sounds, and smells as you do when exploring on foot, but you get to see so much more over the same time period. Turning to camping. It's a neat concept and I really "want" to like it. But when I'm totally honest with myself, sleeping on the ground leaves a lot to be desired, especially for a 55-year-old for whom sleeping is more of an obligation these days than anything. Could an RV or camper be the answer? Maybe. The problem with that is it's just one more "thing" that you've got to store and maintain. What I'd really like is the ability to check into a camper set up on site, fully stocked and ready. A place I could stay for the night and when I'm ready to split, just leave it there with a tip for the chambermaid. I guess they call that a hotel. Bingo. Problem solved!

About 50 or so gathered last month at our home for a resurrected client appreciation BBQ. As the invitation read, my grill stayed covered. I was not going to risk the fire hazard. We brought in Dickie's BBQ, beverages for all ages, and sister-in-law once again baked the tasty desserts. I ordered the weather a month in advance and it came with a picture-perfect winter sunset of oranges, reds, blues, and purples – thank you God. As an added bonus, the International Space Station shot across the sky, thanks astronauts. Now I've been doing this for 20 years and many of you have been around that long. It's not cliché when I call you my client family. We may not share DNA, but we've been through it all. I've seen your kids grow up, make it through college and start families of their own. I helped you transition from the daily grind to a retirement that we'd been planning for years. I've been with you when your job took you away, and been here when it brought you back. We've been sick together, got better, and sometimes didn't. We've been together through the tragedy and heartbreak of losing someone close. I love you guys and there's no place else I'd be, nothing else I'd do. It's the ultimate honor and I am thankful every day.

To the flip side, you've seen my kids grow up, reading about their ups and downs in these pages, often to their chagrin. I've got to report another happy month with Collin in the office. I've said before that I was nervously excited to bring him aboard. I love the kid (you too Alex!) but it was impossible to know if we'd be able to tolerate so much together time. Would it end with a duel? Who knew? So far, it's been anything but. For those thinking about bringing your offspring into the business, here are some thoughts. You should be nervous, it's a big move. That said, like most big moves, its reversible and if you've got an honest relationship, it should survive in any case. The key is to always be honest, and the older I get, the more I value being direct. To twist that shoe-maker's tag line, "Just Say It." As for us, we're adapting to our new, clearly defined roles. Things are more organized and less stressful as we learn to defer tasks to the individual best suited to carry them out. On retirement, I've always said it's not for me. At our Monday morning meeting a few weeks back, for the first time ever, I proposed we plan for this "calling" to outlive Collin as well. We'll see and as always, we'll keep you posted along the way.

Chillin'

Me and my bros

T-ball stars

Alex graduates

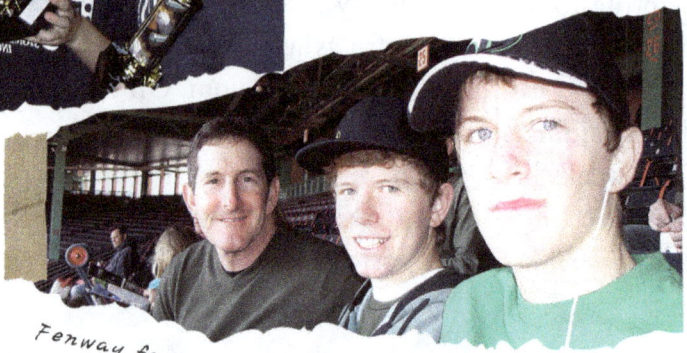
Fenway fans

2020

2020

January 2020

"Be resolute in your goals, but flexible in your tactics."

Jonathan Lockwood Huie

I f the markets taught us anything in 2019, it's that they don't care what we think, how we feel, or what we'd like. A year ago, after the worst December returns in the history of December returns, who would have thought we'd close out the year with the numbers you'll read on the following page? I certainly didn't. But after more than 20 years in the trenches, I had the utmost confidence in our investment process. I knew what we did, why we did it, when we needed a course correction, and what form the correction would take. Our process had us stay the course and we were rewarded.

From Collin: I'd like to start off with an apology. To those of you who have been reading Soundings since its inception in 2008, you probably thought to yourself, "This Collin kid better not come anywhere near my retirement plan!" When my dad tasked me to pen this month's back page, I took a trip down memory lane and read every "On a Personal Note" from the past 12 years. MUST. GET. THERAPY. Lines like, "I've been doing my best to create an environment where my kids would rather hop on a freight train across the country than come back home after graduating", and "The kid may actually end up in prison", brought back some long-repressed memories. Okay, I may have paraphrased the last one but you get the point.

When my folks dropped me off for my first semester of college at the University of Central Florida, my first thought, stolen from Mel Gibson's Willian Wallace, was F-R-E-E-D-O-M! What I quickly learned was this newfound independence, came with personal and more importantly, financial responsibility. I blew through my meager savings within a month and found myself applying for work at the nearest dining hall on campus. To my parent's credit, I was not lacking in work ethic and my past job experience in food service brought me immediate recognition with the boss-man. I found myself quickly rising in the ranks, ahead of folk's years my senior. I can do this. It's not that hard at all to live on my own. Luckily, I quickly realized that "Pizza Chef" was not my life's calling.

Rolling into my sophomore year, I moved to an apartment off campus. Over the years, you've read about my less-than-reliable "wheels." Work was a necessity. I'd grown accustomed to at least 2 meals a day, but limited mobility complicated my employment options. Fate would have it that my apartment complex was hiring leasing ambassadors. I cleaned up, put on a generous slathering of Kagan-charm, and filled out an application. I got the job and with it, a significant discount on my own lease. Win-win. I didn't realize at the time what a great stepping stone this would be. Turns out the best way to pull a quiet, awkward 19-year-old out of his shell is by paying him to talk to complete strangers all day long. And dang if that work ethic, and Kagan-charm ;-) didn't get me promoted to Sales and Marketing Manager. It was a big move financially but more importantly, professionally. Now, I not only had to talk with people all day, I had to create and implement policies, and supervise a team of seven. It was a pretty nice gig for a college student. The money was solid and I had post-graduation opportunities, which took a bit of the edge off.

After graduation, it was decision time. I had been working full time during my senior year. The job was going well. I'd been wined and dined at the national conference in Atlanta and learned about different opportunities in the company, a fairly big regional player in campus real estate. After a lot of thought, I decided that I really wanted to work in a field more focused around my finance degree. You've read that my dad made me an offer, but I'd carved a pretty nice life in Orlando and I wanted to give it a go on my own. After a few interviews, I accepted an offer from an old-line life insurance company. I laced up my big boy shoes and was ready to make a difference! On my first day of training, a fellow employee told me to get ready as they "throw you out to the wolves with little knowledge or training." They didn't cover that in my interview. I found myself constantly calling my mentor for tips and advice on how to make it. He was always available for me to bounce ideas off, or just provide a little pep talk when things felt off. I think you've heard of him, Jon Kagan. After a few weeks of these "coaching" calls, he reiterated his job offer. A few days later, I accepted, and here we are.

I know how lucky I am to be a part of this client family. Like Sandy and my dad, I promise to always be here for you. I hope you are able to look past the image of my middle school days from the Ghost of Soundings Past.

March 2020

"Sometimes, when fortune scowls most spitefully, she is preparing her most dazzling gifts."

Sir Winston Churchill

Without this month's quote-smith, the world would be a very different place. But in his book, "How to Think Like Churchill", Daniel Smith sheds light on some lesser-known facts. His childhood did not portend to future greatness. Like Moses, he had a lisp; like Teddy Roosevelt, he was frail and subject to accidents; and like Albert Einstein, he didn't impress his early school-masters. But like them, and countless others who've been and are yet to be, he became that rare leader, made for his time on the planet, and we are all the benefactors.

When I think back to the years B.C. – before Collin - bringing the kid onboard has worked out in ways that I never expected. Those of you out there who own (or have owned) your own business, know the story. There's no satisfaction quite like the one that comes from growing a meaningful enterprise from scratch. It's blood, toil, tears, and sweat all the way. And it can be a lonely place. Having the kid onboard has added a new depth to the experience for me.

This career is so rewarding and when I do my "Thank you God for XYZ's"...finding my calling lands in the top four. Having Collin around to share the experience has made it so much deeper. I've always loved being a teacher and my son is proving to be a remarkable student. He left school with a degree in finance but when I take the time for some really "deep" thinking, what I'm really teaching him is how to serve. It goes without saying that he's learning how to serve our client family. On top of that, from day one, I've dragged the kid to all of the civic groups that have been important to me over the years so he can see the importance of serving in the community and being a part of something that benefits a cause other than himself and his new extended client family. And he's jumped into the role in a big way. What follows below are some words from "the kid" on some of that service.

"One of the challenges I have had so far in my time back in the Panhandle is getting out from under my dad's shadow. Now I am not saying this is a bad place to be, for some reason everyone seems to like him (probably because my mom is by his side), and I have been given opportunities that I would never have had if not for my genes. My goal is to capitalize on these opportunities and do my best to make sure that the name "Kagan" still makes people think of someone who's out there putting others needs above their own, and maybe even make them laugh with a few corny jokes! Our local chamber of commerce was looking for volunteers to serve on the board and my dad suggested I throw my name in the ring. At the next membership meeting, they passed the microphone to each of us to give a quick elevator pitch. I'd thought one out and sat rehearsing it in my head while I waited for my turn in the spotlight. I pretty much had it down, I was just deciding whether to take my dad's advice and go for some laughs in the closing. It was my turn and as my pop says, "no guts, no glory." I ended with his punchline, "I truly have no idea what I am doing, but I'm excited to learn and give my all to this Chamber", and sat down, happy that I had not made a fool out of myself to that point. Before I could finish that thought, someone spoke out and said "That was great, but it sounded an awful like your dad's pitch a few years ago!" I guess he was so proud of his own speech he wanted to hear it one more time before it left everyone's memories!"

Okay, I'm back, enough from the kid. The back page of this newsletter has always been a place where I open my heart to you all. I know it can be scary…imagine how Kathleen must feel?! But as vital as it is for me to know what's important to you and your family, I think it's just as important for you to know "how I tick". Collin will be a regular contributor here as well with the same purpose. Take care, be well, and talk soon.

April 2020

——————————————————————————————

"In the stillness of the quiet, if we listen, we can hear the whisper of the heart giving strength to weakness, courage to fear, hope to despair."

Howard Thurman

It was 3:55 am when I read the quote above in early March. The market was in the middle of its historic meltdown. I'd just finished my pre-market research and knocked out the Wall Street Journal. The futures pointed to another ugly day. I was letting it all sink in and doing my mental prep for the upcoming day. I took a break to check my email and came across that gem, second in the queue. I had never heard of Mr. Thurman but his words were written for that moment, and reading of his life of service helped put everything in perspective.

A few weeks back, before the lion's share of the planet shut down, I found myself in Orlando for a three-day Rotary President-Elect Training seminar. I was joined by leaders from around the state of Florida and Grand Bahama Island, part of our Florida district. Coronavirus be damned, at the time, Orlando was pretty much open for business. What an experience. There were speakers from around the

APRIL 2020 | 325

globe, my favorite was a young, energetic Brit named Chris Wells. Chris was a character. He leapt onto the stage, pacing frenetically from end to end, as he told the story of how he became involved in Rotary. Despite his boundless energy and enthusiasm, his path to Rotary began with a bit of darkness. He'd recently graduated from university, settled into his dream job, and should have been insanely happy. Instead, he found himself deeply depressed to the point that it became frightening. Two things happened that would change his life. First, a friend convinced him to get professional help. Then, another friend introduced him to Jim Davies, a long-time Rotarian who suggested Chris start up a Rotaract Club (popular in the UK, it's Rotary for the younger generation). Admittedly, he had no idea what to expect but decided it might be just the outlet he needed to give him a shot of "purpose" and help launch him out of his deep funk. The title of his talk was "Do Goodery" and in his words, that's the mission of Rotary. Fueled by Chris's newfound passion, his club quickly starting making a meaningful difference in his town of Market Harborough. They held regular food drives for local food banks, created a support group for young stroke victims, held regular pub quiz fundraisers, and even organized an evening comedy and music event to raise money for a young man who'd been admitted to a prestigious film course in London but couldn't afford the fee. The success of Chris's club was contagious (in the good sense) and several offshoot clubs have sprung up as a result. Good thing. The world sure needs more "Do Goodery."

I love a good road trip and that made it an easy choice to drive down to Orlando for the seminar. Besides the quiet time, it gave me the opportunity to visit my folks afterwards, two hours to the south in Sarasota. My dad had just turned 86, my mom a youthful 79. Growing up, everyone loved my mom. I used to joke that when she walked down the street, the birds would sing, the flowers would bloom… think Uncle Remus. Then came my dad. The flowers snapped shut, the birds dashed off, the skies would grow dark, the clouds rumble. My dad was a tough cat. Small in stature, standing 5' 4" on a good day, he had the presence of a Marine Corps Gunnery Sargent. And he raised us tough, think "Great Santini" tough. He wanted us prepared for the real world. And prepared we were. I actually loved my boot camp GySgt, nicknamed, the "Evil One." He reminded me of my pop. But there we were, years down the road, my pop's memory not what it used to be (who's is). There was a time, spanning around 15 years, when we were estranged, virtually no communication. As such, my pop missed a good amount of my kids' childhood. Now that we are in a good place, I like to share those years and the trials and tribulations that his son got to experience with his grandsons. Payback stuff. During this visit, when I shared with my dad how proud I was of my sons, for the first time ever, he shared how proud he was of his, and what a joy it was to see them grow up and become men. Talk about a lightning bolt. My pop had never, ever shared like this before. Not his style. But as I've said, his memory is a bit in-and-out and during our talk, he'd often not realized that I was his eldest son…hence the beautiful honesty. The Lord works in wonderful and mysterious ways.

As we pass through these challenging times, I'm going to do my best to remember what's most important. Taking care of those we love, not letting anyone slip through the cracks, staying positive and being a part of the solution. The truly wonderful thing about the tough times is that they tend to bring us together, united in a common purpose. Let's see if we can't keep that going after we punch through to the other side. As always, let me know if you need anything. In the meantime, stay well, and cognizant of the many blessings that abound even in the darkest of times.

Finally, I asked Collin to share his perspective on this unprecedented time. Here are his words.

Baptism by fire (phrase); a person or employee who is learning something the hard way through a challenge or difficulty. Just a few short months ago, my dad and I were talking about how great it was that I joined the team when I did. The markets and sentiment were at all-time highs. Client meetings were so upbeat and fun, we were coming off a really great year and there was no reason to think things would be changing anytime soon. My dad let me know that it's not always this peachy. "Just wait till you see a recession. That's when we earn our keep." I shook my head but really didn't give it much thought. We all know what happened next. As stressful as it's been, it's turned into one of the most valuable lessons I could have ever hoped for. We hunkered down with our research, dug into our process, made adjustments to portfolios as the data dictated. I learned more in two months on the job than in all four years of business school. I think I got my first gray hair, and I'm barely 23! But it was an amazing feeling. Our clients (you guys) were surprisingly, pretty calm. We even got emails, calls, and a couple letters telling US to keep the faith. It made me know, more than ever, that I made the right choice in coming to work with my dad, and for all of you. Thank you for your acceptance and your trust. Like Sandy and my dad, I do not take it lightly and every day I step into the office, I strive to be the best servant that I can to all of you. All my best, Collin.

December 2020

"The meaning of your life is to help others find the meaning of theirs."

Viktor E. Frankel

I just finished reading Dr. Frankel's seminal work, "Man's Search for Meaning". First published in 1946, a year after his liberation from the Dachau concentration camp, he explored the traits which allowed some to survive despite such suffering and hopelessness. Inborn optimism, humor, psychological detachment, along with a steely resolve to not give up, were qualities that not only worked in the camps, he wrote, but in everyday life of everyday people facing darkness of their own. He also strongly believed it was our duty to become our best selves. With freedom comes responsibility. He liked to say, "the Statue of Liberty on the East Coast should be supplemented by the statue of Responsibility on the West Coast." Timeless advice for sure.

In a time when much of the national media narrative is focused on bitterness and resentment, it was a breath of fresh air, literally and figuratively, to be out on the parade ground at Camp Bull Simons, home of the Army's 7th Special Forces Group (Airborne). We were there to honor two fallen heroes who gave their last full measure defending the freedoms of those they didn't even know. On a beautiful, crisp and sunny day, hundreds of us came to pay tribute to SFC Javier Gutierrez and SFC Antonio Rodriguez, who were killed in action on February 8, 2020, in Nangarhar, Province, Afghanistan while conducting combat operations.

The ceremony began, as they always do, with the playing of our National Anthem. All stood of course, as all understood what it means, none more so than those in uniform who made up the majority of the attendants. We heard from the Battalion Commander, their unit Commander, Chaplain, and comrades in arms. All were men of honor, duty, courage and service. They spoke openly of their love of God, Country, families, and their dedication to defending the defenseless. It was truly moving stuff that, once again, made me question whether I was trying hard enough on this planet.

For me, the most moving tribute came from SSG Hayden Lloyd, when he spoke to the character of his friend, the fallen SFC Gutierrez. All the speakers noted Javi's (Gutierrez) laugh and overall sense of humor, but Sgt Lloyd told a story that went deep. They were serving together on the streets of an impoverished nation in South America. On the side of the road, as they took a break for a snack, a young boy came to them and asked if he could have some scraps. Javi kneeled down by the boy and engaged him in conversation, the kind of talk that might come from a big brother or "cool" uncle. After several minutes, he took the boy across the street and got him some ice cream. The boy, not used to such attention, did what any young boy or girl would likely do, wrapped his arms tightly around the soldier's neck and cried tears of happiness. (just like I'm doing (again). The world is less of a place in the absence of these two heroes but lucky for us, Collin and I saw hundreds of others just like them. Silent professionals, all.

Kathleen and I celebrated 27 years of marriage on November 27th. I would have never dreamed that my life would have turned out this way. I credit the turn to the partner who steadied my tiller all those years ago. I'd often struggled with depression and the feelings of diminished self-worth that go hand-in-hand. Kathleen's love didn't fit my self-narrative and forced me to gradually change my own opinion of the man in the mirror. We had a nice day, even though a good chunk of it was spent apart (yes, it involved motorcycles). We had a wonderful dinner date at one of our favorite restaurants in Pensacola, the Global Grill. Even shared dessert, a chocolate torte with a little scoop of a crazy-cool, basil-infused, green-tinted ice cream. Carbs don't count on your anniversary.

On the drive home, Kathleen suggested a new "game" when we got home. Not one of those games, we're old. She suggested we each think of two songs that best bring light on our 27-year journey together and play them for each other, alternating back and forth. Isn't it amazing how music can transport you back to the times and feelings you've experienced throughout the years? Obscure songs unique to our history from Paul McCartney, the Crash Test Dummies, Will Kimbrough, among others that made us laugh and tear up, all in a good way, as we "Kagan-danced" the last hour of our special day. Thanks sweetheart, for a new anniversary tradition for this old dog. I love you more each day and can't wait to see where the next 27 years takes us. Maybe dance lessons.

Quick cool down

Happy
go-lucky

12/02/2007

Low
Riders

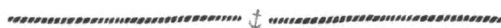

2021

May 2021

It's all about balance. Most of us live frenetically, connected at the hip to our technology, chasing squirrel after squirrel that makes it to our news feed, without giving much thought to our bigger picture. Where am I now? Where would I like to be next year, in three years, in ten years? The older we get, the quicker those years seem to go by. Pink Floyd's Roger Waters nailed it, with his seminal anthem, "Time." Doesn't it make sense to schedule some time, with your partner if you've got one, to plot a course? Financial planning, life planning, call it what you want. It's about living life purposefully and it can be truly liberating.

I recently completed my 57th lap of the sun. All in all, I feel pretty good. If I were a car, I'd say the engine and transmission are better than average, the interior is soiled and worn, the body has noticeable dents & dings and is in dire need of new paint. One thing I've noticed recently is that I've become more emotional. In church, when reading or watching things that tug at the heart, I'm prone to "mistiness". But I'm okay with it. I'm old and understand that what others think of me is none of my business. Besides, my friends and family know I'm still a knuckle-dragger.

That said, yesterday, I think I figured out the cause. Every other day, I run for 40 minutes on our elliptical machine. It's a great low-impact workout, friendly to my wonky lower back, and a better stress reliever than pills. I've got a tv in the room tuned a to Netflix series for distraction. The ideal show will feature a tortured hero, fighting against all odds, for a noble cause. Violence is a requirement, swordplay is best. The thought is that my pain is nothing compared to theirs so I will man-up and push hard. During yesterday's workout, when I found myself getting emotional, I had an epiphany. We are surrounded by so much toxicity, whether it's the news we watch on television, the social media we consume electronically, or the newspapers we read. They point out all that's wrong with the world, humanity in general. It's so easy to get caught up in it all and just resign ourselves to the conclusion that we're all just swirling around the proverbial toilet bowl, destination foregone and unavoidable. Don't buy it. Life is messy because it's filled with humans and we are very messy. Always have been, always will be. That said, there's a lot of good out there, it just doesn't make the news. I see it every time I travel, particularly over the horizon.

Back to my epiphany. I figured out that it's the evidence of this goodness that is literally bringing me to tears. In church, it's easy to find in the words of God and stories from the ages. In my workout yesterday, it was the show I was watching where a band of brothers, united by a common cause, put aside all thoughts and concerns of personal harm to do what was right. In our everyday life, stories abound of folks of all ages performing acts of kindness and bravery for others they don't even know. That's the real humanity. Yes, there is evil out there, always has been, always will be. It's kind of by design. But we need to shift our focus to all that's good and strive to be a part of it. Dang, anyone got a Kleenex?

We spoke with Alex & Claire a couple nights ago. Kathleen called after I read her a story from the WSJ that mentioned Peloton, his employer. Alex and I have the classic, father, first-born son relationship. Could be Freudian. We've always been competitive. I have a great picture of us at the finish line of a 5k race out at Navarre Beach. He was probably 14 or so and we ran together until the last 100 yards. Then it was game on. I beat him by a nose, in my case, a pretty healthy margin. We had clear photographic evidence, but the kid wouldn't relent.

I had a similar competitiveness with my father. Our home was on a cul-de-sac in a modest middle-class neighborhood. In the summer, my dad and I would often bring our baseball gloves out to "the circle" for a game of catch. These are some of my favorite memories of my pop. We'd be out there in the heat, throwing the ball back and forth until one of us would wear out. It was a battle of wills. Would it be my asthma or his bum-shoulder?

Back to the other night. I was tired and cranky and said a couple things that I'd later regret. I thought about it all night and when I got up the next morning, I shot the kid a quick text, apologizing for my ass-ery. His reply came quick and showed once again that the kid's all grown up, and in a way better place than I was at his age. Damn, his mother did good.

June 2021

"Whatever you are, be a good one."

Abraham Lincoln

Here's something to share with your kids and grandkids. There's never been a time of greater opportunity. More than 10,000 people turn 65 every day and many choose retirement. Guess what? They all did something. There is a massive shortage of everything. Plumbers, accountants, carpenters, engineers, white collar, blue collar, take your pick, there's a career or vocation waiting. All you have to do is choose one. Scared you'll choose wrong? Join the club, but it's okay. Just do well and your options remain wide open. Most don't get it right on their first go around but each choice gets you closer to your ideal. But you've got to act.

I'm the first-born son of a last-born son. Often leads to trouble. At one point, we'd gone about 12 years without speaking before I picked up my cell phone with nothing to lose. That was about 12 years ago. We're now at the best place we've ever been. It's a beautiful thing, except my pop has Alzheimer's.

I just came back from visiting my folks in south Florida. My mom, always a Saint, has been a loving and dutiful caretaker for the past five years on his journey with this awful affliction. In the beginning, she said that she loved him even more as is often the case when caring for a sick child. But she's exhausted. Caregiving for a loved-one with dementia is a full-contact sport. I'm not sure where we'll end up, but we're working on charting a course that is best for everyone.

It was a wonderful visit. Growing up, my pop was a man of few words. He rarely spoke of his childhood. His folks emigrated from Russia. I'd never met his dad, none of us had. He'd passed before my folks ever met, when my pop was just 28. His mom, Celia, was with us briefly. My last memory of her was a visit to a nursing home in NYC but I was not much more than a toddler. Until this recent visit, I'd never even seen a picture of my grandfather, Max.

In his current state my dad, if nothing else, is talkative. At this point, it's pretty much a circular conversation, often with himself, repeated over and over. On this visit, he shared an important piece of his upbringing. In one conversation, it was as if he'd gone back to his early teenage years. He spoke of his pop getting on him about "things". He never got into what things specifically and when asked, he was pretty vague (as he was on all the subjects we touched). That said, when I probed about his feelings towards his old man, the tone of his voice and sparkle in his eyes said it all. He'd had a solid childhood, with loving parents and he wished he had let them know how appreciative he was. I told him then, that as one of his sons, I can attest for myself and the other two that we felt the same and we loved him dearly. I don't know that he understood who I was but none-the-less, it brought tears to my eyes when he replied, "You're a good man." Love delayed is some sweet love for sure.

August 2021

During their 2004 round-the-world motorcycle journey, Ewan McGregor and riding partner Charley Boorman struggled mightily in the relentless terrain of inner Mongolia. They considered a detour which would relieve their struggle, but they'd miss an important stop in Ulaanbaatar. They dug deep, persevered and made it to their destination where they visited an orphanage that changed Ewan's life. It was there he met and later adopted a young girl, he and wife Eve's third child. In his latest moto-documentary, the "Long Way Up", the actor gave an emotional testimony of the life-changing consequences of pushing through fear and adversity.

Shortly after returning from Colorado, I joined my brother Jay, back down to Sarasota, Florida to visit our folks. Our mission was to put a plan in place to get my dad the care he needed for his dementia. We had a lot of anxiety going into this trip. My dad's mood and behavior were so unpredictable and my mom was becoming overwhelmed after nearly four years of constant attention, made infinitely worse by the isolation of the pandemic. We had two main goals. First was to get him to his appointment for a memory care assessment, a requirement for the second goal; to visit some local facilities and select the one that my mom was most comfortable with. I'm happy to report that the mission exceeded expectations. Dementia is different with everyone but so far, my pop is mainly very positive. He has the same conversation, over and over, every day. The gist is what it means to be a "human being" and to help your fellow man. For most of our visit, he likely didn't know that Jay & I shared his DNA, but he none-the-less, enjoyed our company and knew that we were there to help. After four productive days, we accomplished all we'd set out to do and we hope to get him settled into his new digs within the next few weeks. Mom is relieved and the wonderful facility is only a few miles from their house. Thank you, God.

September 2021

Reading the first paragraph of "The Mountain Shadow" was like reconnecting with an old friend. I was truly sad when I finished "Shantaram", Gregory David Robert's first book. The 900- page behemoth tells his story, the escape from a maximum-security prison in Australia, and his subsequent adventures on the run in India. He hooks you from the very first paragraph, and if I had the time and stamina, I'd have read it in one sitting. "The Mountain Shadow", its sequel, picks back up in Bombay and it's equally gripping. Part philosophy, part travel journal, all adventure, Roberts paints a picture like few others. You can see, smell, and feel the story as the characters and the settings come alive on the pages. Rumor has it, there's a series on Apple TV in the works starring one of my favorites, Charlie Hunnam. Keep an eye out.

Kathleen turned over another digit in the odometer of life. We've been together nearly 30 years, miracle of miracles as far as I'm concerned. I was disappointed with my orders to report to Pensacola. As always, God knew better.

I reconnected with an old friend from flight school and months later, accepted an invitation to dinner where his wife told me about a life-long friend of hers whom I had to meet. She described a fit and attractive woman, a big runner, who had a solid career and owned her own home. She was my age and had never been married. My initial reaction was something like, "Sounds like the Easter Bunny. What's wrong with her?" "Bad choices in men." said Tessa. "I've got a chance!" I replied and so began our adventure. Thanks sweetheart, for giving "the Navy" a chance.

October 2021

We are what we think. Unfortunately, for many of us, past trauma has set the baseline for both where we are and what we believe is possible. The good news is that with purposeful effort, we can change. But it's up to us. I read a wonderful testimonial from a man who found redemption through Alcoholics Anonymous. "Once I realized it was up to me, I made the choice, and the healing began." Twelve step programs add in a huge dose of spirituality, ultimately important in my opinion. But if that's not your thing, substitute karma, Zen, or any force outside of yourself that brings you strength, peace, and comfort. A great book for anyone looking for guidance is Dr. Benjamin Hardy's, "Personality Isn't Permanent."

A retired couple came in to discuss funding options for a new home. They had more money than they'd ever need, and no bad options. Husband had one idea, wife had another, and they were looking for a tie-breaker. What made it so interesting, was the background conversation. The wife told us she'd had an NDE. I admitted I didn't know what that was. "A near death experience", she replied. She had a bad fall while at a doctor's office, hit her head, and was in a very rough way. A classic out of body experience, as she hovered above the situation, she felt HIS presence. "Are you ready?" He asked. "Thy will", she replied. It turned out, it was not her time, and she came back, to continue life forever changed. In the transformation, she learned that there is no need for fear or worry, God has it all. We continued our discussion and landed on a solution that took both parties major concerns into account. As for us, we pay the bills by managing assets, but it's meetings like these that are the most rewarding.

Zero-hour was approaching. Kathleen and I arrived in Sarasota on a Friday night and checked into the hotel room that would be our base-camp for the next 5 days. We'd spent the weekend getting dad's room in the memory care facility all set up and it looked great. Planning complete, it was time for the execution. Our anxiety-meters were off the charts. Dad was so unpredictable. He cancelled appointments all the time, and the prior day, got pretty upset when he awoke and found me and Kathleen in his house. Our hotel had a Starbucks on-sight and when I made the trip for morning coffee, I decided to share my feelings with the young barista. She was surprisingly knowledgeable and encouraging, telling me of her friend's grandmother receiving wonderful care in similar circumstances. It's amazing how God puts just the right people in our path.

Pop awoke in a good mood, a great sign. Mom had him up and ready when I arrived at their place. We sat at the kitchen table and talked for a bit, our standard ritual over the past several years. My dad would start slightly combative, not knowing who this strange bearded man sitting across the table was or the nature of his intentions. As we talked, he loosened up, and we loaded into my truck for the short drive to the facility. Our plan was to get to the facility just before lunchtime, show my dad his new digs, and have him join the other residents for lunch. Kathleen and I had met Jack, a resident, over the weekend when we set up dad's room. We told Debbie, the ALF chief, and she thought he would be a good person to introduce to dad at lunch. During the drive, dad and I continued our banter, laughing and joking, he was in a good place mentally. Debbie met us as we entered the facility and we took a walk to pop's new digs. He loved it, and I talked him through all that we had done. We walked to the window and talked about the wonderful view of trees, and down-sloping lawn. We moved to the cozy siting area, TV and picture of Babe Ruth in a Red Sox uniform, donated by our Collin. I jumped on the comfortable bed and noted the beautiful picture of the beach that would be the first thing he saw when he woke up in the morning. Then came the moment of truth, the hand-off. I told pop that mom had to go away for a few days to care for a sick friend with no other family. He'd be staying in this wonderful place, with these nice people, and everything would be just fine. There was no resistance. Debbie led dad to the dining room while we stayed back to use the restroom. Dania, one of the nurses, came by and we briefed her on dad's general condition.

Five minutes later, Debbie came back to the room and said dad was doing well, sitting with Jack and another resident, nicely engaged in conversation. As we followed her to her office to complete the last of the paperwork, we stopped to observe dad in his new home. He was across the room, back towards us, but we could clearly see that things were going very well. In Debbie's office, I was moved by a picture on the wall which read, "It's not our workplace, it's your home." After 3 days of interactions with these remarkable care-givers, it was very clear that they lived by that mantra. We finished up with Debbie, got in my truck and I checked my watch. Amazingly, we carried out the entire plan in just under 40 minutes. My mom, summed it up when she said, "I can breathe again."

EPILOGUE

It's been quite a journey. I sure hope there's much more to come. Our boys are men, but they've not yet given us grandkids...no pressure, kids. Kathleen and I will celebrate our 30th anniversary this November...thank you Bob and Tessa...and thank you sweetheart (you are going to heaven for sure!)

Folks often ask me about my own retirement. I'm on the cusp of my 60th year but have no intention of riding off into the sunset. I love what I do. It is my calling and it's who I am. With Collin onboard, it's even more special to know that our mission will long outlive my years. As for this book, we're years away, but I've already got a sequel in the works. "Son of Soundings: More reflections...", which will feature a lot more from Collin and possibly even Alex, who we hope takes us up on the offer to join the firm in the future.

Some final parting advice on how to navigate the ups and downs of our "try out" on planet Earth; Work hard, Be humble, and as my role model and current pastor says, Love God, Love your neighbor. The rest seems to take care of itself.

And to many more!

ACKNOWLEDGMENTS

When Collin joined the firm in 2019, he decided to go through all the old Soundings to get an idea of how our clients might feel about his career move. He became a little concerned after landing on an old missive where I noted something to the effect, "The lad may end up in prison, but if so, he will rise quickly to cell block leader." I've had fun with this thing over the years and need first, to thank all who ended up in its pages, for tolerating me. I love you all.

As for toleration, my beautiful wife Kathleen is truly a Saint. For more than thirty years, she's been my best friend, soulmate, WAY better half, and right hand. Sweetheart, you are the love of my life and to me, irrefutable proof of the grace of God.

I thank my parents, Joan and Jerry Kagan for their love, beatings, and guidance over the years. I earned the beatings and they made entry into the cold, cruel world, a relatively benign event. We were certainly not an "off-the-shelf" family. More the Bunkers than the Cleavers, my brothers and I were raised to know that we could achieve anything we worked for but were entitled only to the right for its pursuit. I love you guys and thank you for everything, scars included.

To Alex and Collin, our sons who've survived plenty of beatings of their own, we are so proud. You've grown into such solid young men and you bring us more joy than you could possibly know. Your mom and I believe that all love is "tough" and if we left any scars, remember…chicks dig them.

Finally, to everyone in our client family. We love you and think about you more than you imagine. This is way more than a career for us; cliché as it sounds, it's a calling. We strive to become better every day so that we can, in turn, serve you better. There is nothing that we take more seriously and personally, I thank God every morning for the blessing of being a part of your lives. This is not something I'll ever retire from. I can't say that Collin won't one day change the locks at the office, but if so, I'll figure something out.

ABOUT THE AUTHOR

Jon Kagan is the President of Soundside Wealth Advisors, specializing in comprehensive financial planning and investment management. Naval flight training brought Jon to Pensacola in 1986 after graduating summa cum laude from the University of Massachusetts with a bachelor's degree in business administration. He served for 10 years in the U.S. Navy as an officer and helicopter pilot, deploying from both coasts and serving in Operation Desert Storm. While in the Navy, Jon earned his master's degree in management from Troy University.

Jon lives in the Florida Panhandle with his wife Kathleen. They have two grown sons. Alex, an accountant, lives in Boulder, CO with his wife Claire, a doula. Collin is his partner who joined the firm in 2019 after graduating from the University of Central Florida with a degree in finance. Jon is a past president of the Navarre Chamber of Commerce, and past president of the Rotary Club of Navarre serves on numerous non-profit boards and is a Mentor in the Take Stock in Children Program. Jon also authored the book, You're Gonna Make It: The Indispensable Guide for a Woman Facing Divorce - a compelling resource that supports women through every stage of the divorce process and shows them that renewal is not only possible, it's inevitable.

DISCLAIMERS

[1] Insurance policies have exclusions and/or limitations. The cost and availability of life insurance depend on factors such as age, health and the type and amount of insurance purchased. As with most financial decisions, there are expenses associated with the purchase of life insurance. Policies commonly have mortality and expense charges. In addition if a policy is surrendered prematurely, there may be surrender charges and income tax implications. Guarantees are based on the claims paying ability of the insurance company.

[2] The foregoing information is not a statement of all available data necessary for making an investment decision, and it does not constitute a recommendation. Any opinions are those of Jon Kagan and not necessarily those of Raymond James. Expressions of opinion are as of this date and are subject to change without notice. There is no guarantee that these statements, opinions or forecasts provided herein will prove to be correct. Investing involves risk and you may incur a profit or loss regardless of strategy selected.

[3] While we are familiar with the tax provisions of the issues presented herein, as Financial Advisors we are not qualified to render advice on tax or legal matters. Raymond James does not provide tax or legal advice. Please consult your own legal or tax professional for more detailed information on tax issues and advice as they relate to your specific situation.